"Live your life as when you die….

… you wish you had lived!"

-Anonymous

Disclaimer

The information in this book is for educational purposes only and is not intended to be a source of professional advice. Readers should consult with a professional where appropriate. The author and publisher disclaim any liability for any loss or damage resulting from using the information in this book.

The content is not intended as a substitute for professional medical advice. This book is based on the author's memories. While efforts have been made to recount events accurately, some names and details have been changed to protect the privacy of individuals.

Introduction

Across the years, those acquainted with me have frequently proposed I author a book, acknowledging that my observations have resonated profoundly within them and touched upon their most guarded sentiments. There has been persistent praise for the lucidity and eloquence of my prose, but the accolades, I maintain, belong not to me but to the Spirit that inhabits me. This Spirit, not the conscious mind, guides my words seamlessly to the page. Every missive herein serves as a lesson for myself and those engaged with my work. The decision to transcribe these insights into a physical form was not borne of ego or self-gratification; rather, it was an offering of myself and a journey to our Heavenly Father and His Holy Spirit.

Many have pointed out the instrumental value these contemplations hold in the interpretation of their own lives. Thus, this book was born out of consideration for their feedback. The book encompasses two core sections that interweave with one another. I christened learnings, observations, and thoughts "Gleaned Insights from Gnostic Exploration," which collate the wisdom amassed through experiences of enhanced consciousness bred from metaphysical events, dietary disciplines, and fasting practices. Subsequent chapters try to relate and make sense of the Metaphysical events throughout my life, ultimately convincing me to share these lessons and events with you.

This work is dedicated to my terrestrial father, whose guidance remains with me: "A man is not complete until he plants a tree, has a child, and writes a book." My identity today is the result of his unwavering encouragement and influence.

To my father, I offer my heartfelt gratitude... Thank you for the crucial role you have played in my life.

The audiobook rendition of this compilation is lovingly devoted to my girlfriend. Her presence in my life confirms that the journey to a destined end can transpire through various routes. Moreover, she exemplifies the notion that preferred mediums of information intake can vary - some prefer to imbibe the messages through listening rather than reading.

Thus, this treasure is presented to you in dual formats—written and audio—in the hope that it will reach and enlighten all seekers.

SAVI

Conversations With Spirit

A Call to Be

We are already what we must be

What is there to do, to be, to have?

Where does the power of the being reside?

If that which you already are is perfect and complete

and a part of you,

Why strive to achieve something else?

Is there any solace in the outcome?

Or is the journey of discovery the art of creation that

which we are after?

Questions unanswered become the beacon home.

Where is home?

Is that a place or a feeling?

Are we inside ourselves or outside looking in?

What is the true nature of reality if it is perceived by the filter of our assumptions and the color of our interpretations?

Who is the accurate observer within the center of our being?

Who am I? What am I? What am I here to accomplish?

Am I different?

Am I missing something?

Am I capable of accepting myself?

Am I all that I can be?

Am I being enough?

I am that I am...

I am nothing, yet in that emptiness, I discover the perfection in my imperfections.

I am everything and everyone in that which we share the same.

The same heart, illusions, and aspirations

The same seeking after that empty, missing piece within our core which we seek to fill from the outside...

Only discovering that in that vast emptiness within us is the Spark of creation itself.

The Light that self-ignites to quench all the darkness...

Once I bid in this Light, I can see my true self, perfect and complete from the beginning of time..

Once I become that which I already am, I am free from the illusions, the seeking, and the mortality of my fragile self to be One with my Higher Self..

I remembered why I came here to be.

I remembered who I have always and forever truly am.

I see you, I feel you, I am you...

Just Be,...

LOVE

SAVI

The First Encounters With The Unexplainable

Not making sense of the perceived reality in my early years

Let me simplify it and confirm that I am crazy, so you don't need to question my sanity. I've already done this for you, so there's no need to resist what I am about to share. With this essential clarification out of the way, I invite you to abandon all preconceptions of what is realistic and what is not. It took me decades to muster the courage to openly admit to myself and others all the experiences I will share throughout the book, interlaced between higher awareness teachings, observations, and thoughts.

It all started on a gloomy winter day in Buenos Aires, Argentina. I was about six years old, gazing out the window of my bedroom on the fourth floor of our modest apartment in Belgrano, when I heard what I would later understand in life was the voice of the Spirit within each one of us. It spoke so vividly that I still recall it as if it were yesterday. It was not like the incessant self-talk, the 'psychopath within,' that all of us experience until we calm the neural patterns through transcendental meditation. I digress, but this voice was more subtle, with an ethereal presence of complete stillness and peace. Unlike the constant self-talk, this voice seemed to originate from a much deeper realm of which I was then unaware. It felt like it originated outside of me, yet the voice was not directly audible; it was more like a telepathic experience. It sounded akin to an older man, which was strange, considering I was only six years old. One thing I was certain of: It wasn't my voice.

I heard out of thin air, *'I will leave you alone now, but you will find me again...'* Without a clue, I was first taken aback and looked around to see where the voice was coming from. I was alone in the room as my mom was far away preparing supper that afternoon. Once I regained my composure and subdued my initial fear, I asked, *'Who are you? Wait, don't go...'* to which I felt what I could only describe as a loving presence and a sense of infinite comfort. Then, in what I could describe as a telepathic exchange, the presence asked me what I wanted to achieve in this life. I provided a simple answer that, little did I know then, would guide the entirety of my earthly experience—being brought up Catholic, my early childhood innocence requested from the presence that I wanted to get to know and follow Jesus Christ as this was what it was being taught to me in school and by my family. The presence then imbued in my awareness its assent to my request, and I felt it as it departed.

To this day, I have no clue what transpired, who or what that presence was, how even to describe it, or any of the implications of the exchange. My life went on. I had a difficult childhood for many reasons that are not important to bring forward. However, frankly, today, I see them as the cornerstone of the man I have become, allowing me to explore unconventional means of existence while being of service to others.

I was still young when the next event took place. To provide some context, we had a beautiful one-hundred-and-twenty-five-acre weekend house that had been in the family for three generations. We used to gather on this property, which boasted a substantial two-story estate built by my great-grandfather Manuel and a smaller, more quaint home built by my grandfather Oscar, which I will mention later. During the summer months, I would spend my school breaks mostly living in harmony with nature and communing with horses, cows, chickens, and dogs, experiencing an immense sense of belonging and peace. I didn't recognize how blessed I was during those early days, having the opportunity to experience this communion with nature away from the city. There were hundreds of over-forty-five-year-old trees on the property, which Manuel himself had planted when he acquired the site with the foresight of creating a private country club one day. Unfortunately, as is often the case in families, after great men come weaker ones who don't dare to follow through, so this plan never took place. My father was not allowed to make decisions as he was not a relative by blood, and the family members in charge, although well-intentioned and possessing integrity, ran the family fortune into the ground due to their weak leadership character and incompetence. It was during these summer days that I developed a severe case of warts growing both on the left side of my foot and on my right hand. I have always been empathetic and somehow have a heightened sense of awareness, which put me in a constant state of internal turmoil in those days. By then, I had already experienced severe bullying at school, given my awkward demeanor. Additionally, let's just say that my parents' disciplinary modality involved the good old belt and demanding results, all of which added to my internal self-conflict. These parenting methodologies, which would be unacceptable in today's views, likely contributed to the stress. It is my guess that everyone attributed these warts to my heightened stress level and decided to remove them surgically as they continued to grow and were causing me pain when I walked.

After what seemed to be a routine procedure, all the warts were gone, but to everyone's surprise, they came back with a vengeance in the same spot. By then, everyone, including the doctors, was a bit taken aback, as the procedure had gone as planned, and what they called the root of each wart was removed in a fairly deep incision. Somehow, they concluded that this was a psychosomatic event, and I needed to convince myself that they were to be gone for them not to grow again. So, my parents, in their level of awareness, told me a story that involved me believing that the warts would go away on their own. This involved rubbing a small piece of pig fat on each wart during a full moon night and burying said piece in a red ant mound. Once the ants finished eating the fat, my warts would disappear. As Dr. Joe Dispenza would attest, the power of perception and the mind is yet to be fully understood, as is our healing power and supernatural abilities. In my childhood innocence, I was convinced that I would heal naturally on my own. I monitored the warts, and within a few days, overnight, I woke up, and they were gone. Now, it is hard to comprehend this, and I still have my questions. However, I can tell you that I had another more vivid supernatural healing event involving my lower back in which, fully conscious, I felt the presence of the Holy Spirit heal my body, which could be construed as a true miracle. I will wait to go into these details. I want you to open yourself to the possibility of the unknown, understanding that there are forces in this reality that we still do not understand or fully grasp. The human condition is a miracle; we are all much more than what meets the eye.

Moving on in my timeline, I had the opportunity to live a somewhat ordinary early life within the confines of a typical family. Other than the sternness of my parents and their narrow-mindedness as to what and how my own life ought to be lived confining me to a very demarcated lifestyle, I had no other issues. We were living in the northeast US due to my father's career when I decided I had had enough of the US lifestyle and wanted to return to Argentina to pursue my university studies right after graduating from high school. I moved back to attend engineering school in Buenos Aires while my parents and brother stayed for another year. During my second year, all my family had already reunited and settled back, and we lived together in a new home in a subdivision known as Belgrano. It was then that the next inexplicable metaphysical event happened.

I discovered that our Father in Heaven has a very talented and, in specific ways, sarcastic sense of humor. I have such humor; hence, He reflects my sense of humor to me in a way that I can relate to. So, there I was, and it's hard to forget when physical reality decides to change itself or the laws governing it to show you something you have yet to experience. I was given the awareness of the irony of the event decades later.

While studying Newtonian Physics during my second year of formal engineering school, the Divine decided to show me in a very vivid manner that humanity doesn't have a clue about the true nature of the dimension we live in and that the only Laws of the Universe are the ones dictated by our Father in Heaven as His will can instantly mandate the breaking of every physics law known to humanity in the material realms. On to the point I have been avoiding thus far, I had my physics book open one afternoon, trying to make sense of the equations. I had just finished drinking a can of Coke, which was on my desk by my side. Before everyone here starts assuming alternate explanations, let me provide more details. All the windows and doors to my room were closed, so no air currents were plausible as we did not have central A/C like here in the US, which is not customary down there; my ceiling fan was also off because it was autumn. Now, I witnessed the following event with my own eyes, and only a few years ago was I able to make peace with what I am about to share.

Without my intervention, the Coke can flipped on its side, rolled onto a perfectly level desk with a glass top, and fell to the left side. I dismissed it immediately, thinking I had accidentally bumped it, and you may also draw this conclusion: I do not blame you if you did. So, feeling a bit spooked by what I had just witnessed, I got up from the chair and looked for the Coke can on the floor. Despite spending two hours completely dismantling my bedroom, to this date, I still couldn't find the can. It had seemingly disappeared from the physical 3D plane. I had no choice but to put the event in the back of my mind and forget about it. Later in life, after experiencing even more transcendental events, including apparitions, I understood that I was being prepared slowly throughout this journey to be ready to understand other planes of interdimensional existence, including what we call life after death and the existence of an overarching Divine presence to which all of creation bows, not out of fear, but out of gratitude for Its unconditional love for each one of us and everything within all its realms.

Journey to Self-Discovering the Ultimate Truth

Who are we in the eyes of others?

Although you do not know me, based on what I've heard, I feel I know you simply because I see a reflection of myself in you. Let me assure you that there is no judgment on my part in any of the words I write here. I am merely sharing my soul with you, heart to heart, as I've recognized many aspects of myself.

You probably think it's crazy for me to write this letter—and yes, perhaps it is a little—but there are no worries here. I am just being true to myself and who I am in Spirit. When I see a courageous soul entering its Divine, Rightful Presence in this 3D world, my integrity compels me to show up and be of service.

First, allow me to commend your courage in seeking the ultimate truth by exploring further and feeling the call to continue your healing journey. But you are struggling with one final lesson: understanding one of the three pillars of life's existence on Earth. Let me offer you a different perspective to help set yourself free.

The first and second lessons are two sides of the same coin for many reasons, as we fundamentally are all One. Unconditional love for yourself is the same as unconditional love for others. What you resist and dislike in others is what you cannot accept or forgive in yourself. The issues you experience in interactions with coworkers or close family members reflect this last lesson. Once you recognize that everyone carries their childhood wounds, burdens, and challenges, failing to release and accept everything as it is in each soul's journey, your Ego begins to dictate how things should be. In this dichotomy between what seems to be (which is never the complete truth) and what is happening, as well as the conflict between your aspirations, pain takes root. Stop judging everything, including yourself. Conflict cannot exist unless you emphasize duality through judgment. The ultimate truth is that life is a 3D simulation where every circumstance is ideally crafted to benefit our Spiritual Growth. Nothing else matters; eternal gratitude for even the most challenging lessons and injustices is the key to manifesting unconditional love—for those who wrong us and, most importantly, ourselves. There is no other way to free yourself back to your natural state of Being Divine, which allows everyone to exist without judgment.

Look at your parents, regardless of whether you feel love or disdain for them, as emotionally wounded six- or seven-year-olds whose parents also hurt. The pain they cause you or your siblings is the same pain they experienced growing up and have not yet managed to acknowledge and heal. We, the Light Workers—courageous souls who agreed to come to Earth and manifest our Father's Heaven through us as portals of Love—are challenged to heal up to seven generations of prior karma by sharing unconditional love and empathy. I understand it is daunting, especially as your amnesia does not let you recall this agreement. But remember, nothing is by mere consequence; everything is by design. You chose to attend the Earth School and embark on this Soul Experience. You selected your parents and your lessons, so STOP complaining about the curriculum and start LOVING every moment of it.

Allow yourself to be free of all preconceived notions and imposed social constraints. Stop worrying about who you must be or think you are and start simply being. You are already complete and perfect; even your imperfections have existed by Divine Agreement and Design since the beginning. No amount of tools or sacred medicine will bring this awareness unless you allow yourself to be free. Whenever you place expectations upon reality and others, you bind yourself and them to your Ego. Stop trying to steer the course of your life, and instead, take the passenger seat, allowing the Spirit to guide you.

I love you as I love myself unconditionally. I welcome you to our home for as long as you need to find the ultimate truth of who you are.

An Unexpected visitor one night

The most essential, when least expected

Nothing much had happened since the prior events until the latter part of 2001 when I moved from California to South Beach for my last corporate job. Having been recently let go due to what could be characterized as the beginning of my Calvary, I had begun to experience the pressure required to change from my old self into the blossoming of the being I am today. I can't express my gratitude to those who dared to steer me into the abyss of the unknown and for their unanticipated contributions to my life's journey. After what had been a stellar initial corporate career at a very young age, I was now faced with having to make ends meet with no savings and looking at the possibility of homelessness. All while confronting the necessity of self-sponsoring a working visa and finding a way to attain my legal permanent residence in the US. During the day, I would work on the company's business plan and immigration papers and study for my real estate license, as it was the only opportunity I could find within 90 days of being let go to remain in the US legally. I had just deposited all I had left of my savings after paying for my MBA in Berkeley to acquire the apartment I was renting as the whole building was being converted from rental to condos, which was a thing those days. I had no credit, and the interest rate I paid for my one-bedroom was over eight percent. The level of stress was gigantic; I barely had money to eat, and I had to do labor work in construction during my free time at nights or weekends, such as painting apartments by myself in the building I was living in, which would allow me almost to cover the monthly mortgage and expenses. Why is all this important? I emphasize that divine intervention in the physical planes of existence is possible and a reality for those who are open to it.

About six months have passed of this tortuous existence. Somehow, I attained my real estate license and found the means to survive. I was working roughly 16-hour days for seven days a week non-stop. Despite these demanding hours, I even saved approximately twelve thousand dollars. This money was used to renovate my now-owned apartment with the intent of flipping it for a tax-free profit within the next two years. All I had to do was to continue the pace and, somehow, survive. I had a goal and saw the end in sight, albeit a distant future. Those days, I used to be so driven that I could overwork anyone. My ego and drive were such that I knew I could take on whatever the world would throw. I hired an Argentine general contractor who was licensed and renovated the building. He assisted me with the permits, additional labor, and materials. With a properly executed contract and all my belongings placed in the bedroom, he demolished the entire kitchen, living room, bathroom, and entry foyer. At the same time, I went to spend Christmas in Argentina with my family. Of course, I left him with the capital required for the work to progress throughout that month, so when I was back, the idea was to move from the bedroom into the finished living area and then tackle that room as the last item of the renovation. My bank would not allow for non-presential wires, so sending him the money every week was out of the question, and I had no one else I could entrust for oversight either, as I was new in town. By then, we had established rapport and explored the idea of going into business together, renovating other units, or eventually developing them. So, I trusted him with the task and the capital.

My trusting nature believed in all his progress reports and advancements. I did not have an iPhone then, so it was not like I could do a Facetime or Zoom call. To my nasty surprise, when I came back at the beginning of January, the apartment was almost the same as I left it, with no real advancement to speak of, and the contractor was avoiding me at all costs. Later, I found out that he had developed a cocaine addiction and was spending his nights frequenting South Beach nightclubs. I was left with the daunting task of finishing the work myself and with no capital, as I had already given the money to him. It was one of many lessons of betrayal by contractors and later other business partners in Miami in this industry that I categorized as conniving at best. I state all these facts because I was at my breaking point when the next miracle happened.

Sleeping amidst all the dust and the ongoing renovation, in a wedge of the bed surrounded by boxes and personal belongings, I worked myself to exhaustion from sunrise to sunset while also renovating the unit. I couldn't afford to pay anyone, so I learned how to do drywall, tiling, and basic electricity and plumbing. I asked another general contractor to oversee my work to ensure it was done within the building code, as I needed to pass inspections to close the open permits. However, because there were no significant alterations, the construction was straightforward. I vividly remember that the apartment was finally done by the 4th of July, while the fireworks were going off at 9:00 pm. All I needed to do was apply a fresh coat of ceiling paint. I was up on a ladder, painting, when I suffered my first lower back episode.

For a reason unknown to me, something went wrong with my spine, likely due to both the physical and mental stress, and my vertebrae pinched my nerves. An excruciating pain, equivalent to being stabbed in my lower back with a knife, shot through my body. I fell off the ladder and ended up on the floor, unable to breathe, let alone move. There I lay, alone on the floor, looking at the kitchen counter where my cell phone was out of reach, unable to scream for help. My Red Cross lifeguard training kicked in, and I reminded myself that it's panic that kills people who are drowning, not the water. I realized that I had to breathe, no matter the level of pain. Slowly and steadily, I forced myself to stay conscious, or I would pass out. The muscle spasms that had forced my spine out of place eventually subsided slightly after an eternity of thirty minutes. I managed to crawl onto my bed slowly. There, I cried; the despair was so unfathomable that I was confronted with the idea of ending it all then and there.

Here comes the good stuff, but before you can understand the relevance of what comes next, I need to provide additional background information so that the following miracle will have the same significance to you as it did for me.

A few great men were in my family; one of them was my great-grandfather Manuel and my grandfather Oscar, whose name I carry as my second name. Both men defied the odds, achieved significant wealth by different means, and earned societal recognition. My great-grandfather Manuel was an industrious accountant for a wealthy family and constructed a small real estate empire that sustained several generations. On the other hand, my grandfather Oscar was a self-taught salesperson who eventually became an industrialist with a passion for cars and some real estate development.

Within my family, I had the living example of the story 'Rich Dad Poor Dad' by Robert Kiyosaki through the lives of my great-grandfather, my grandfather, and my father. Now, Oscar was an extraordinary soul. I never met him; he died of his second heart attack at the age I am now, 52, because his closest family member bankrupted him by stealing from the factory. Oddly enough, speaking of generational karma, I experienced the same these past few months. Still, luckily for me, although I had a chest episode when given the news that I had just been defrauded of all my capital by those closer to me to whom I had extended my hand and resources, my heart was strong enough to withstand the event.

Anyway, back to Oscar, whom I never met in person, but I encountered his legacy instead, learning how fondly those who knew him spoke of him. He was widely known for his acts of kindness and assistance to others. One of the most significant moments during my childhood was when my mom's cousin, effectively a second uncle to me, who had been put in charge of my grandpa's factory, gave me a tour.

I met one of the janitors who had worked for my grandpa Oscar during this visit; this person was one of the oldest employees, and I have had a lot of interactions with him. As my uncle introduced me, "This is Santiago, the grandson of Oscar." I vividly remember this man's eyes almost watering, and the words that later came out of his mouth defined the persona I wanted to embody and one of the most profound spiritual lessons of my early life. "*What a great man your grandfather was; he has helped so many...*" Statements such as these from him and others showed me early on that the critical aspects of a true man's legacy are not wealth or forceful victories but the legacy of what others will think of us when we are no longer on this earth. Right then and there, I made the resolve that I wanted in my life to be of service to others, and whatever I ended up becoming, I wanted people to remember me for how I was instrumental in their life's journey once gone.

So, back to that night in South Beach, as you will now understand its relevance. I had a vivid dream as I fell asleep crying in despair at my situation. In that dream, I was standing on the porch of my grandfather's weekend house at night, overlooking the vast and beautiful five-acre gardens. A huge party was going on, much like the one we had with over sixty people in my childhood. Everyone was having a blast. Some appeared to be speaking, and others were even dancing. Curiously, it felt as though I knew them all, but their physical forms were all in their early thirties, making it hard to pin down who was who. This surprised me because I didn't realize I saw all my ancestors together; some would look at me from afar and smile. As I write this sentence, I have tears and chills running down my spine. I have only shared what I will tell you with a select few. I could sense a presence to my left, and as I turned, I saw a young, thin, medium-height man looking at me with piercing dark brown eyes and a smile. In a very calm and soft voice, he asked me how I was and what was happening. Innocently, like a child, I responded that my life was a disaster and that I wished I was dead. The level of physical and emotional pain was so intense that my body was shutting down. I didn't see how I could go on, given my current circumstances, and couldn't see a way out. I felt cornered by life, unsure of how to move forward. Also, I expressed that all I wanted to be when I grew up was like Oscar, my grandfather, a self-made man admired by others who left a legacy of selflessness. The person beside me smiled; his eyes sparkled with what I can now describe as the joy of a proud father looking at his son. Then he tells me, "Everything will be ok, wait and see." He warped his arms around me in a warm hug. In that dream, at that very moment, I experienced absolute bliss. My pain disappeared, and for the first time, I felt what I didn't know then was unconditional divine love. As the man pulled away from me, his face morphed into that of Oscar's, just as I knew him from the old photograph I had of him at 52.

Now, what is so significant about this dream? You may describe it as a vivid dream, and yes, based on what you know thus far, you're probably right in your assessment. But here is where the magic started: as Oscar pulled away, I suddenly woke up, still feeling this immense divine love, yet unable to breathe. I tried reaching for my phone on the nightstand but was completely paralyzed. The alarm clock showed it was 5:00 am. Lying there, I thought I was dying; my back had probably snapped; I was now paralyzed and couldn't breathe any longer. I remained calm as I was expecting to lose consciousness and pass away.

Meanwhile, I was experiencing what some call amor-fati and this overwhelming divine bliss. After what felt like another eternity, similar to the previous night, I sensed a presence leave my body. As this presence departed, my body regained its mobility. In a brisk yet careful move, I sat in bed and took a deep breath. As I gasped for the air, the presence was leaving, as was the blissful state. I looked at the alarm clock again; it was now 5:03 am. Through some miraculous event, I was still alive and had managed not to pass out despite not breathing for over three minutes.

I managed to get up and compose myself. My new working bathroom allowed me to prepare for the day ahead as I had a rental showing in Key Biscayne. I intended to close a rental contract that day to be able to pay the prior month's mortgage and building maintenance. Brushing off the previous night's dream and the strange event of the morning as delusions brought on by the stress I was under, I went on with my day, still barely able to move due to my back injury. I knew something wasn't right with my body, but I didn't have health insurance or the time or money to see a doctor. This was going to be just one of many instances where I would be confronted with life-threatening situations and potential insurmountable medical expenses in this life journey here in the US. Meanwhile, my family back in Argentina were unaware of my perils. Yet somehow, life seemed to straighten itself out, and miracles took place in each of these instances, but these are not examples I care to share.

As I was driving over the Key Biscayne causeway, I received a call out of the blue. Out of respect for their anonymity, I won't refer to any third parties in this book. I will also avoid mentioning direct details as this book, if fallen into the hands of those close, may inadvertently hint at the participants. But the call went like this: "Hi Santiago, you probably don't remember me, I am... You introduced me to... six months ago. I don't have to do this, but I want you to know that I made $250,000 thanks to you, and I want to give you

10% of it right now." I had to pull over to regain my composure; my hands were shaking, and my heart was pounding.

My prayers had been answered, but more importantly, I realized that something much more significant had occurred in the last few hours and that the vivid dream was more like a spiritual visitation. I'd asked for a miracle, and God had answered. Overwhelmed with emotion, I called my mom. Without detailing all my troubles, I told her that her father, Oscar, had worked a miracle for me. Never underestimate the value and power of lending someone a hand; you do not know what they are going through and to what degree you are being of service. Remember this story the next time something with you raises your awareness of acting kindly. In essence, you are an instrument of the Divine in your small way in the great tapestry of life.

This was the first of many instances in which, through divine, timely intervention, the material needs of my journey were provided for. You may dismiss these two stories as mere coincidences, the overactive imagination of a distressed individual, or stress-induced neurological hallucinations. I am not sharing my most intimate experiences for you to judge, although I know there will be many who will. I am mustering the courage to share all my metaphysical experiences so you may open yourself to the possibility that they may exist in a form and dosage perfect for each circumstance. If you only expect to categorize miracles as the apparition of the Virgin Mary or some sort of Angelic Being wielding a flaming sword and calling your name, then you are missing out of what else could be available awaiting your discovery.

Through The Eyes Of a Child

The Truth behind childhood traumas

I haven't met yet one being that has not suffered from rejection through their childhood; many of us have not received enough love and care from others as we once would have hoped. It could have been our parents, guardians, siblings, or even others in our circles. Some may have been the victims of brutal bullying abuse, like me in my early years of school, attacks so vicious and threatening that made us fearful and make us develop a defensive personality in which we portray ourselves to the world as strong, mean, a nobody tells me how and what to do philosophy or what may be even worse, some self-defense mechanism that we instead attack first than get hurt once again. Meanwhile, deep inside, unconsciously, we crave acceptance and feel completely unworthy of love because of the mirror that the world has shown us at a young age. We, deep inside, somehow develop a feeling of not being enough or missing something. We think or perceive that the world will finally accept and love us once we figure out what it is.

Well, I am here to tell you that after five decades in this journey, I assure you that nothing outside of who you already are will take this feeling away. It was by acts of Grace that I discovered the journey into self-love, most importantly, unconditional self-love, which allowed me to, in return, reframe all my past emotional injuries from a different perspective. Make amends with the perpetrators in person and my mind and "heal" the emotional wounds. I know that many people go to therapy for decades trying to overcome these, and others resort to addictions to numb the unworthiness that causes the pain inside. Many others try or fall prey to modern or old alternative therapeutic activities with some degree of success. But frankly, nothing outside us can direct our emotions toward a constructive outcome of Spiritual Growth. All Religions are deceiving; there are significant truths in all, but unfortunately, all point to dead-end roads in which one is left aspiring for salvation that somehow a merciful God will impart or that there is a need for countless rituals or ceremonies to attain an altered state of being and somehow becoming Worthy in the eyes of everyone and even God. Some go as far as claiming the physical transmutation of the human being into light matter through ascension, which I do not negate, but that as an objective is flawed and to my point. I have been a witness to most of it all in my quest for the Truth. I can tell you that through my Spiritual journey, I was granted a pick behind the veil of this reality first to heal myself and then help others heal themselves. I asked to know the ultimate Truth, and recently, last year, I was shown in a vision the answer through an expanded momentary state of consciousness during which the answers were revealed to me by Grace. Making sense of these truths, I am now pointing a flashlight into the darkness to see some of these aspects for ourselves. As the beam of the flashlight can only make us see a piece of what is in front of us on a dark night, so is the capacity we presently embody to hold the totality of God's Truth and the reality of the Game called Life.

I can attest to the miraculous nature of this Universe and the existence of Ascended Masters, which are mentioned in all religions, including Jesus Christ. I have eye-witnessed the presence of the Holy Spirit with my two eyes three times in the same way described in the New Testament. Most importantly, I have witnessed a Demon myself and the Power of the Word of our Father in Heaven, and I saw His Holy Light by my side with two blinding eyes like Moses. I hid in the shadows for over 20 years, trying to understand everything. Thinking I was going crazy and justifying myself as simply having seen hallucinations until miracles happened around me, which were events of such an implausible probability that my scientific mind could not make any sense of the defiance of the fundamental laws of physics. Mater disappearing, objects levitating, spontaneous healing, Holy Spirit Tong Speech, Christ Consciousness, among others.

In short, I am here to tell you what has been revealed to me: that the only way to heal your experiences is to accept them, release the grief, and let go of the identification that these things happen to you because you are not enough. All these events, as atrocious as some may be, do not happen to you; they happened for you. They are invaluable life lessons purposely designed by our Creator to experience precious lessons that guide your Soul's development journey to a higher level of enlightenment. You will always hear me say, "We are already perfect and complete," I must giggle because I am not supposed to cheat and give you the end-game results; we play with ourselves. But the truth is that the higher the spectator's vantage point, the smaller the difficulties seem, as you see the much bigger picture behind it all. Once you know we go on, everything is perfect and complete, so God allows things to happen as they do. The closest analogy is that your Parents do not wake you up if you are having a nightmare; you experience it like in a virtual simulation, and after a few hours, you simply wake up and brush it off. There are, again, many similarities to the analogy of what life is for our Soul or Spirit.

As Jesus Christ taught, we are all but One in Spirit. Unfortunately, one of the biggest lies perpetrated by Religions is that somehow, we need intermediaries between us and God. The placing of His only Son at His right hand casts the rest of humanity or non-believers into a simple lower-tier existence for all eternity. Although Jesus Christ has a special place both in History and Heaven, Jesus Himself will tell you once you meet him that He is but of service to all of us with infinite humility and His Father our God has as all in His Heart at the same level of Love as expressed on an apparition - vision to a dear friend of mine one afternoon. Of course, there are those that God chooses for a purpose more significant than others, and within this selection, there are the ones that heel to His call and accept.

Well, I can tell you that the Love God has for each of his creations is only rivaled by His Love for Himself, as God is not but Love itself. For those who need to hear this, it is essential to open your eyes, hear and remember. We are all created in His Image. There are significant hidden Truths behind all of this. But how dare you not Love Yourself if the Creator of The Universe already Loves you unconditionally, just as you are? Like an old friend of mine once told me, "Who do you think you are?". I didn't know that answer then, but I know it now.

My last hint is that as much as many in the world question the existence of God or even many of the Masters before us, I can only laugh very hard knowing what their faces will look like (figuratively speaking) right after their deaths as they not only get to realize that they move on into a different dimension of consciousness and regain some if not all of the totality of their true identity while losing all their Egos and earthly identifications. All of which, in a sense, were not real at all. Depending on their evolution, they can meet face-to-face with other Spirits in the forms they are ready to assimilate. The ultimate truth revealed to me is not for the world to know yet, as many are not even awakened from their slumber. But I tell you that God is playing the longest and most beautiful game of Hide and Seek throughout Eternity. That His Love is beyond our current earthly comprehension. That there is not a second of existence that has not already been contemplated and that every possible solution to your dilemmas has already been enacted. The game is for you to realize this truth and surrender the control of your life to His Will. The most significant act of Love a child can have for a parent is to say, Daddy or Mommy, I want to be like you. How would your life be like if you wanted to be like God? What would God do if He/ She would walk this earth in human form? How would God treat each one of us? How would you treat each other if you were God playing in a dreamlike state, being yourself? Questions that point to hidden Truths.

What if, for a minute, Jesus Christ's teachings were a bit different than what we have been force-fed? What if the actual message He came to tell us was. Hey, wake up! We are all Sons and Daughters of God, and in this mystery lays the key to the Kingdom of Heaven. What if the only thing we need in our lives is to let go of trying so desperately to make ends meet, push to be driven to total exhaustion, and return to a more balanced existence with Nature while fostering a socio-economic system that contemplates not a cut-throat competition in a winner takes all, but a cooperation of sorts instead? Unfortunately, we have tried many experiments as a species in a social construct, and in my humble experience and opinion, all the prevailing systems we have ever tried have failed. And don't tell me that capitalism is perfect either; we live in a nation that should be embarrassed of itself. With over

45 million souls below the poverty line and the last I checked, over 650,000 homeless, if not more.

Meanwhile, we spend trillions on war-industrial machines that only benefit a few and are utilized as an imperialist tool under the disguise of protecting a democracy, which has become a joke in a two-band circus of revolving clowns seeking power capable of betraying all moral standards for a sip of temporary power. A legislative system is burdened with frivolous laws in a litigious society with a total loss of any moral compass due to the selfishness instilled since childhood during early indoctrination. The phrase "You reap what you sow" applies also in this case.

You may ask whether the last paragraph has anything to do with spiritual teaching or even this open letter. My short answer is everything. Through the eyes of a child, we are wounded, and we continue to wound others as we helplessly seek to heal that wound. We try to attain more and more identifications outside ourselves and strive to feel enough. We continue the quest regardless of the consequences when we do not feel worthy. If we have a weak moral compass, we resort to cheating and lying to advance and finally buy the material things or experiences we presume will make us complete. We are willing to kill, steal, rob, torture, and whatever the most depraved act you can think of, all in pursuit of an exterior thing that will fill the gaping hole inside.

However, very few realize through Grace that it is a fruitless game. The famous actor Jim Carrey once stated, "I wish everyone could get everything they want so they realize that is not the answer." The good news that I am here to tell you is that I managed to experience Gnostically the Truth of who and what we are, and I decided to do my part to help everyone brave enough to face themself to achieve the same. There is nothing I or anyone can teach you because you already carry all the answers inside your being, so I do not seek followers, fame, or even fortune. All I can do is stand at the highest mountain peak and scream with all my might that the Truth is Within you. I can point at it from afar. The journey is personal and within yourself. But I have the great news that once you seek the Truth, the Truth seeks you back and claims you as its Own. There is no religion, ceremonies, classes, or Gurus that can change you simply because you are already where you need to be, and frankly, you are already enough, Worthy, and Complete. It is in this, one of the ultimate Truths, that you, yourself, will release the wounds from childhood and make this wonderful Earth a better place for all of us to live in.

Once the Truth opens your eyes, there is no going back or keeping quiet. Someone can't accept the current situation in every society in the world. We are not meant to come and experience labor slavery while a few gorge on their riches. We are more than simply the titles, positions, wealth, and power some claim for themselves. Do I advocate that there is no merit in hard work? No, there is; not everyone should receive the same, but I also see a rigged system in many ways that only very few can crack by simple circumstances that many times are serendipitous. I know that most rich, self-made people like to see themselves as the party responsible for their success.

Still, the truth is no man or woman alone can accomplish anything meaningful in one lifetime if not by the conditional or unconditional support of many.

I always asked our Father why I had been abused in so many ways during the past decades, and the answer was short and straightforward. So you will be ready to judge your brothers and sisters who are prepared to enter the Kingdom—understanding today that our Father's Kingdom is not a physical place but a state of expanded consciousness which one can only attain by His Grace and the true meaning of Jesus Christ's Communion or Last Supper that very few get. The whole point is that once we surrender and let go of ourselves, we allow our Father to be in communion with us. And through this, we get to experience the magic of His Kingdom, albeit temporarily, as we ascend in our own Spiritual Journey. Jesus Christ managed to attain this in a sustained manner. His teachings reflect hidden absolute Truths, some of which I highlight in this writing. I am nothing special; I am like you, a wounded child who once thought I wasn't enough or worthy of love. I carried a deep hole in my inner being, which I tried to fill with material experiences, things, or others. I was quick to hurt others before they hurt me again. And I am telling you that there is another way. Drop your shields, drop your exhaustion, and stop allowing others to tell you how and why you should live your life a certain way. Stand for the Truth no matter the consequences while you seek higher hidden ones. Never bend your knees for your fellow brothers or sisters, as we are all at the same level in the eyes of our Father. No single one of you is less than any of the others. We are all perfect and complete, even as broken as we may seem. We can all be redeemed if we ask Heavens to be so.

We are all in a magical game of hide-and-seek with our True Nature. And with that, I tell you... love yourselves unconditionally the same way I learned to love myself. I also love and accept you for who you are, not how you may think you are.

Random Events Leading the Way

Exploring the Unknown: The Initial Willful Encounters

As with everything good in life, it starts small and when you are not looking. My first encounters with the Spirit were random and in a time and place, I least expected. I vividly remember the events but not necessarily the exact chronology between them. As I expressed throughout other passages of this book, I never lived an extraordinary life; if anything, my desire to attain freedom from all my childhood family impositions always drove me to seek escape from constraints. With this, I chose a life more steered towards freedom and travel than a career path. My real estate brokerage practice allowed me the flexibility I aspired to attain this freedom. It was never easy because being a solo practitioner within my brand made it significantly more complex than if I had gone to work as a salesperson or broker within the top brands. I digress, but I wanted to set the tone for this chapter as the subsequent events' time and places differ from your typical nine to five.

I am not sure why, other than my thirst for exploration and, frankly, instinctive drives, which led me to establish a relationship with a friend of a friend in Santa Cruz de la Sierra, Bolivia. Again, to protect the anonymity of others, I will not provide further details. Having connected with this individual and fostered a lovely pen-pal relationship for some time, I discovered that we had many interests in common. So, one day, out of the blue, I decided to travel to Bolivia as there were potential business opportunities in the region in agriculture toward the later part of the 2000s. While there, I was able to deepen my knowledge of the area and said opportunities while strengthening my bonds with my new friends.

One afternoon, I had the chance to accompany them on a ministry mission within their church to a less-than-favorable neighborhood in town to deliver some donations. The Jeep van we were driving had seen its heyday long ago and could be considered a rust bucket—nothing uncommon in developing countries, but certainly not what you would be driving in South Beach. I have never been a man to shy away from a good adventure, so I went along. I remember that day perfectly; when the supernatural becomes natural, you tend not to forget. By that time, I was beginning to develop what I like to call "*a connection*" with the other side, or Spirit, through which I would empty myself of all thought, find stillness in my mind and heart, and somehow not ask myself how—simply because neither I understand it nor know how or why—I would feel a sort of energetic connection with what I have come to call my Higher Self or Spirit. In this connection, I know that what I ask is given to me for the benefit of all those involved, and all I say is, "Thank *you.*"

With this clarification, here are the events I recall: we all went inside the building where we needed to deliver the supplies. As we came out, my friend, who was in the driver's seat, tried starting the vehicle, but it did not prevail. She had almost drained the battery when I told her to stop and let me check the engine to ensure no connections were loose; I have always been a bit of a car buff, like my grandfather, Oscar. I enjoyed playing mechanics in Argentina, but I always got my hands dirty with tools and engines. Anyhow, I opened the hood and checked the battery connectors, the relays, and the starter. Everything seemed normal. I knew that the engine had just worked. We were not out of fuel as we had over half a tank, and I could see the carburetor spraying fuel. I checked for sparks by unplugging one of the harness's leads and checking for ignition. "*Uh oh,*" I said, "*we are in trouble now,*" as nothing obvious was happening. I noticed my two friends' anxiety starting to ramp up to a heightened state. I asked them why they were so nervous, to which they responded that we were on the wrong side of town at the wrong time, and if we did not leave soon, we would undoubtedly get mugged. Our lives or wallets were at stake. With this, I asked my friend to give the starter another try, and if the engine turned over, she should carefully pump the gas to ensure we had enough fuel; we waited to see if the engine was flooded—being warm and at high elevation, that could also be the reason. Again, she cranked the engine several times, but after many attempts, nothing; the battery was indeed beginning to deplete, making the engine slow to turn. We had been at this now for over thirty minutes.

Then, something came to me: a total stillness and certainty. With this embodied state, I asked my friend to let me sit at the steering wheel. I closed my eyes and rested my hands over the steering wheel; I "*connected*," as I like to call it, and made an intention. It was simple, "*Please start.*" The air was thick with anticipation, and I could feel the tension in the car. It is hard to describe the feeling once I know my intent has been fulfilled, but it is one of absolute certainty. I said, "*Thank you,*" merely a few seconds after my friend had tried in vain for over thirty minutes. I turned the ignition key on, and the engine rumbled to life instantly, the sound of its awakening echoing in the stillness of the neighborhood.

It is hard to quantify this as a miracle, as there was no supernatural event one could pinpoint, but it was one of the first times I had experienced the synchronous connection between mind, heart, and the wish fulfilled. Everything I share in this book results from my gnostic experiences with inexplicable forces and circumstances. There have been other instances like this, but I prefer to save space for the truly remarkable and unquestionable ones, which I will discuss towards the end of the book.

Let's focus on a more supernatural event to start warming you up for the ones that will genuinely leave you gasping for air. I can't just jump to the deep end, or I'm afraid I might lose you. It was a typical workday; at the time, I had bought my dream waterfront condo on an island in South Beach, and I was finally living the dream. I had an excellent work-life balance that allowed me to walk from my home to a gym that was located above the Sardinia Restaurant in Maurice Gibbs Memorial Park. So, there I was, at the gym in the middle of the morning. As always, when I least expected it, the unexpected and supernatural decided to show up. Between training sets, I walked towards the water fountain as I was, for whatever reason, extremely thirsty, more than usual. As I approached the water fountain, there was this colossal guy, your typical professional bodybuilder.

I mean, his arms were the size of my legs, to put it in perspective. He was crouching over the water fountain as he drank, taking his sweet time. The amount of water this man was drinking, and the time he was taking, made it seem as if he had just returned from an expedition in the Sahara desert. I was starting to get annoyed; I was desperately thirsty by now, and he just kept crouching over with the water now hitting his lips and spilling over. I contained my annoyance and said to myself, "*This dude is huge; I better keep my cool; we have nothing to prove here today.*" In what was almost perfect timing, as Divine Timing always is, the minute I surrendered and simply let go of my desire to drink, this man stood up. His eyes were red from crying, which I had not noticed; he was emotionally disturbed and shaken. Given what I was witnessing, I didn't understand what was happening before me. I went from being annoyed to feeling concern and empathy for him. Before I was able to muster a word, right when I was about to ask him, "*Are you okay?*" he burst into tears and told me, "*God himself is telling me to tell you that He loves you very much...*" To my surprise, with my jaw completely open, I stared at him, and for a brief instant, we locked eyes. I felt his presence and knew he was not lying to me. I hugged him and whispered, "*Don't worry, you're not going crazy*"; this sort of thing happened to me, as this was neither the first nor the last time our Heavenly Father channeled through others in plain sight to deliver messages to and for me.

This man, who I never saw again, was so embarrassed about crying in front of everyone in the gym that he gathered his belongings and ran away that day. I never saw him again, but I know for certain that this had to be a defining moment for him as much as it was for me. I brushed off the event as I normally would and continued living an "*everyday*" life, if such a thing existed for me.

Losing is Actually Winning

Once we lose ourselves from our intent, we are free

We have all thought that winning is about achieving something we aim for or don't have, but today, I want to share with you that the most significant realization and blessing we can have in life is the opposite of what we are taught in childhood.

Losing is winning. Although the pain arises from the dichotomy between desired expectations and obtained circumstances, those who are "blessed" by life to continuously fail, lose, or even flounder ultimately, emotionally, and economically, have the power to realize and understand the deeper meaning of those mentioned above. Losing is truly winning and a blessing.

When life takes us on paths different from those we set out on, it forces us to reevaluate the ideas of who we believe we are and what we think we should be. From childhood, we are forced and indoctrinated to live under specific criteria and parameters that mark a fictitious initial course that is socially acceptable and seems aspirational from the start. But the reality is that maturity is reached the more one errs and fails to adjust existence to those expectations. 95% of people conform to accepting these social and existential structures, adapting to live a so-called standard life with lesser or greater degrees of sacrifices and achievements. There is nothing wrong with this, but the remaining 5% never find solace in living in such a way.

Those who achieve moderate and gigantic professional and economic successes are considered heroes. Those who do not achieve this are relegated as failures and forgotten. But today, I tell you that although it seems that my reality is the latter, I want to leave you with the knowledge that there is only peace in my soul, that I am a witness of a living God, that the Holy Spirit has manifested itself around and in front of me three times just as God himself showed his presence visually and audibly to prepare me and give me the Faith and conviction that what He has prepared for me is 100 times better than any of my failures and that He will give me my place on this earth.

For this, I must stop trying to control my destiny and finally accept, surrender, and trust that everything will be for the better. Therefore, with all the blows and failures over 28 years of suffering and sacrifice, today, on my 52nd birthday, I publicly declare that I am one of the most successful souls to have walked this earth. I have surpassed all expectations and trials that have led me to learn the true purpose of life, to answer who and what we indeed are, and the reality we come to know, which is to love everyone and, above all, ourselves unconditionally while finding that at the center of our Being is the Temple of the Divine Spirit.

None of these conquests, which cannot be measured at first glance, could have materialized in me if I had not learned that Losing is Actually Winning... When one loses something, one realizes, among several things, how valuable or not that something was; if one has the opportunity to recover it materially or emotionally, one does what is necessary to make it so. Otherwise, one takes stock and lets it go, knowing it was one of life's many lessons for our emotional and spiritual development.

Detachment is the greatest blessing someone can achieve in a lifetime. When one detaches from the identity one tries to show or achieve, one opens the door for reality to guide us to manifest our true human potential, leaving behind all social and mental pre-conditioning. This leads to finding unconventional methods of existence and truths hidden in plain sight.

In my life, I have interacted with many people of unimaginable economic levels capable of moving a finger and fulfilling any perversion or dream in a matter of minutes. So far, I have not met anyone who was happy with themselves or felt fulfilled internally. In the loss of everything we cling to, we finally see that our value is not tied to externalities of our being but is a Divine right innate to us that we come to experience in this simulation called Life. We are all Divine beings having a three-dimensional experience with amnesia that forces us to think that the tangible is the only actual reality when behind these dimensions, there are even higher superimposed ones that govern them and indirectly us.

Therefore, today, I tell you that those who genuinely learn that losing is winning and that all those who rob, take away, or reject us are doing us the most tremendous favor possible. They allow us to cultivate ourselves in ways I cannot describe. They help us become genuinely indestructible and achieve absolute peace; it's like being completely naked in the street without fear. Knowing we are Children of God and that we have a mission ahead far greater than any of our human dreams. It returns us to our natural essence, indestructible even by death itself. Beyond what our minds can comprehend, there exists a liberation and happiness that manifests within us when we free ourselves from all material and aspirational attachments, allowing us to experience what remains of our lives from a perspective of total and true freedom. Freedom to decide where, how, and with whom to live without mental preconditions of what is or isn't acceptable.

A free being can manifest from his true nature since we resonate with our interdimensional essence, which we call "Soul," without having a complete vision of what it is. But just as the law of gravity causes a body to fall if released in space towards the Earth, and even more than 337 years after Isaac Newton mathematically published the observations of this, no one truly knows why and how nor the interrelation that ties it with space and time. We accept it as accurate within known parameters, but it is not the absolute Truth; it is just an interpretation that makes sense to the perception of reality. In the same way, some forces shape us and lead us through unknown paths outside of known parameters.

It is for all this and even more that I can briefly share today; I want to convey these words to all of you, the most valuable beings God has given me in this life. So that you may have the same peace in your hearts that I carry and understand how grateful I am to all of you for being in my life, expect the unexpected from now on as a normal condition in my existence because, from today, I have made the resolution to affirm my Divine right to be Free from all impositions and preconditions and, most importantly, to let my soul manifest from now on and not my Ego. From now on, our Father is in control of my destiny; I intend to pursue not the material but the experiences that the material provides me. To live each day with total detachment from outcomes or conventional ideals. I desire what remains of my life to let everything flow and let the most outlandish dreams manifest if they are meant for me.

Therefore, today, I toast all of you for the greatest gift God gave me: the Freedom of myself and the courage to manifest it. Let these painfully learned lessons be my gift so you may also dare to express the true greatness you are aware of within you.

I love you unconditionally.

Facing Off With the Demonic

Choosing Between Light and Darkness: A Crucial Turning Point in Life

Here we go; buckle up because until now, I have been beating around the bush. In this section, I will share something that will undoubtedly have you gasping for air by the end of the chapter. We are going full supernatural on this one. This was the first time out of three I experienced the presence of our Holy Father and His power. By the end of this section, there will be no doubt in your mind that there is more to what Christianity and Catholicism teach us about our relationship with this entity if we can call it that. However, there isn't a word encompassing the totality of the reality we call the Divine. This reality is personal and up close, requiring no intermediation.

It was just a typical Saturday night in my early thirties. I was invited by one of my closest friends, with whom I had gone to school in California and who later moved to Miami Beach, to visit the apartment of someone we knew. This was a beautiful place overlooking Biscayne Bay; the night was warm, and the stars were shining. We arrived and commenced mingling. I have never been much of an alcohol drinker, as it is not something that resonates with me, but I sporadically enjoy a glass of good red wine on social occasions. So, it is rare for me to drink at all, but at this event, as I went to get a glass of red wine, a lady approached me out of the blue and started interacting with me. I don't quite remember how we hit it off, but our conversation quickly turned from small talk to her wanting to know more about Christianity, particularly the life of Jesus Christ.

Looking back, I didn't see any red flags. It might seem odd that someone would ask about such a topic at a Saturday night party out of the blue. However, since she mentioned she was Jewish and was considering getting baptized, she asked if I could provide some information. There was nobody else at the party that I cared to speak to, so I chuckled and told her exactly, *"Listen, it's funny you should ask. I was brought up Catholic and went to Catholic school all my life, but frankly, I'm done with religion and God. He has abandoned me lately, and I am going through an agnostic phase. Let's go out there to the balcony, and I will share what I've been taught. Why not?"*

The conversation continued for hours; by around twelve-thirty at night, most people had left, and the host politely asked if we would also go. Now, here comes the beginning of the saga; this lady had expressed over the past few hours that she was suffering from severe depression and was experiencing suicidal thoughts. Having been in similar situations myself, I couldn't in good conscience let her go without doing my very best to alleviate her pain and hopefully provide enough emotional support to give her a new perspective on her predicament. So, I suggested we walk back to my place, which was a short midnight stroll away, where we could sit on the outdoor hammock by the water's edge, overlooking the night sky, and continue discussing the Virgin Mary, Jesus Christ, and the Catholic Church that she was so inclined to learn about. She accepted my invitation, and we continued our conversations during our walk and at the water's edge near my building until three in the morning. By then, I was exhausted, and I stated, *"I am Jesus-ed out,"* and suggested we call it a night and that she should head home.

To my surprise, she didn't want to end it there; she expressed a desire to wash my feet, which left me utterly perplexed, as this had never been offered to me before. I hesitated, unsure of what exactly to say. My masculine instincts took over, and I had to politely decline her offer, as I was not physically attracted to her. She quickly asserted that she wasn't trying to make a move on me but that in her religion, it was traditional to wash someone's feet as a show of respect. I later learned that the symbolism of washing someone's feet in Judaism is multifaceted, reflecting a blend of hospitality, humility, respect, and religious ritual. This practice, deeply rooted in ancient customs, carries significant historical and spiritual meanings of which I was unaware. For the priests in the Israelite community, washing their hands and feet before entering the Tabernacle or approaching the altar of burnt offerings was a mandated ritual, symbolizing the need for purification before performing priestly functions or approaching the divine. This ritual underscored the importance of cleanliness and preparation in religious observances, drawing a parallel between physical cleanliness and spiritual purity. In the context of what was about to occur, it made all the sense in the world. Also, a free person willingly washed the feet of others; it was seen as a profound expression of friendship and humility. This foot-washing aspect underscores the values of servitude and humility, elevating the act to a gesture of deep respect and care for others.

　　With all her insistence, I conceded, and we went upstairs to my home. I prepared a bucket with water and a towel. We had only had one glass of wine each, and just to be clear, I had never done any psychoactive drugs till that day. So, we were not under the influence of any substance. I sat by the edge of my bed, dimmed the overhead lights, and lay back as she kneeled before me and washed my feet. Whether you believe a single word of what I am about to share transpired next, I beg for your humbleness at heart to keep an open mind and treat the event with the solemnity it deserves. Opening and sharing these facts with the world is challenging. Still, as part of my journey and integrity, I feel compelled that it would be incredibly selfish of me to die without sharing everything in this book before the end of my lifetime, as it may help others renew their faith and seek the unknown.

Well, here it is then; as she was washing my feet, she looked up at me, and what I can only describe as a transfiguration of her face occurred. A dark, swirling entity or demon appeared. This thing started talking to me in what sounded like an ancient language, which I couldn't even replicate today if you asked me to. Incredibly enough, I could understand every single word as this entity spoke. There I was, sitting on my bed at three in the morning, with a demon holding me by my two feet, speaking in a language I didn't know I even knew, and I understood his every word. Let's pause, breathe, hold that thought... ok, let's move on.

This entity provided me with a recapitulation of the disaster my life had been till that day and all the pain and suffering I had been encountering till that day, which is irrelevant to your knowledge and the message behind this passage. But let's just say that if Satan sends one of his team to pick you up and offer you every single one of your life's desired unachieved goals, it is a highly tempting proposition. Once the demon had stopped speaking to me, I was petrified. I was trembling in fear, and I was of the mind that I would shortly meet my demise, thinking that whatever was in front of me had the upper hand, and like we say, I was toasted. All I could muster was the strength to die with dignity and honor. I remember as if it would be happening right now. I screamed from the bottom of my soul. *"NO"*. At that very instance, the fireworks began in the room. What I could describe as being plugged into a high voltage line or the equivalent of being hit by lightning, my whole body began to vibrate at an extremely high frequency. I felt the presence of an energy I can't even put into words. I remember seeing my hands shaking and feeling as if my chest was about to burst open. And it happened; I did not understand it then as I was petrified in fear, but later realized what it was. Our Holy Father answered through me back to the demon in that ancient language. With just but a few words that went something like this: "*Leave my Son alone, or I will come down and destroy you...*" This entity came out of the woman's body, crawled through the wall and ceiling of my room, and exited via the window. What looked like a long black tether from the back of the humanoid form connected to the woman's heart. Once this was severed, the lady fell to the ground and started shaking, screaming, "*I don't want to die...*" repeatedly. I swiftly jumped from the bed, crouched, and held her in my arms. She was paranoid; it was like a spell was broken, and she was waking up from a nightmare. You could see in her eyes the sheer terror.

I did my very best to hug her in a firm embrace as she cried inconsolably. I told her, "*I got you; you are not dying.*" Meanwhile, I was still in shock and kept an eye on the window, praying that whatever that thing was, it wasn't coming back. While still in my embrace, the lady looked at me and calmed down; she then asked if I would baptize her. Being Catholic, I remembered that in cases of extreme need, I had the right and power to do so. So, I asked her how she wanted to be known and proceeded to baptize her. By then, it was well into the early hours of the day, and we remained still until we both regained our composure and agreed that we would not share with anyone what had happened that day. I have kept my promise until this very moment. Still, I have taken the liberty of sharing this with only a few brothers and sisters in the past that I knew it would be instrumental in their journeys, and now with the world, as a radical shift is needed in humanity to finally claim their Divine Sovereign Rights over the darkness ruling this world.

If there's anything to take away from this passage, it's not how courageous or extraordinary I was. What is within me is within everyone who has ever walked this earth and ever will. Again, I am nothing special, and I choose to be a vessel for the Spirit to be of service; that is my only claim to fame - being courageous enough to go against societal norms. But the lessons are that we are all Sons and Daughters of the Light and that our Heavenly Father loves every single one of us. He will move Heaven and Earth to protect us spiritually when we desperately need it. So, do not buy into the scriptures stating that only Jesus Christ is divinely cared for or any other religions steering you away from the core of what truly resides within your deepest core. You are a walking, breathing Tabernacle; our Heavenly Father is as much within you as in heaven.

We are all exceptional and must only claim our Divine Rights to walk in His Light. Remember this the next time you feel unworthy or beaten down by life. Everything is an illusion, and only you can free yourself from bondage. Wake up!

Our Relationship with Pain

The hidden Guru within guiding us

As humans, we are preconditioned to avoid both physical and emotional pain and seek pleasure. From childhood, we are constantly confronted with opportunities to experience both, and as we age, many of us still do not appreciate the subtle differences between pain and suffering. Unfortunately, this leads to the constant seeking of pleasure outside us via different means while trying to avoid pain. In the most distorted of these outcomes, many resort to compulsory behaviors, which in the extreme may result in various kinds of addictions, from mild to truly devastating.

All of us need to understand that pain is, in fact, a necessary aspect of the human experience, and the constant avoidance of it may be depriving us of one of the most enriching experiences of our lifetimes. All types of pain are unavoidable, from physical to emotional. We will experience it whether we want it or not. The rationalization of this critical fact is the cornerstone for understanding that a spiritually mature individual will, in fact, welcome and embrace pain because it is, in a sense, a compass showing us something that may not be in complete agreement with our lives. On the physical plane, pain shows us a discrepancy between reality and our bodies, pointing us to take corrective action to reverse the course that has led to the pain. In the case of illness, we are forced to take better care of our bodies, which are temples of the soul. In the event of emotional pain, we encounter something similar but with more profound implications, as it forces us to mature emotionally and, first and foremost, accept what is and is not. Both types of pain open the door for a deeper understanding of the optionality of the temporary pain caused by circumstances or the permanent suffering caused by our ego's non-acceptance of what is versus what we expected. In a nutshell, when we realize and accept that most situations in our lives that have caused us pain are entirely beyond our initial control—due to a lack of awareness of the factors that initiated the events and/or the exogenous forces working against our will—we finally allow ourselves to break free from the continuous necessity of accepting suffering as a condition.

We seldom control what enters our lives and do a mediocre job managing it. As humans, we tend to see reality through the filters of our senses and our expectations of what it should be instead of simply allowing everything to exist without creating labels. I have seen many people emotionally recover from irreversible physical conditions such as amputations and become more robust versions of who they were. I am no stranger to physical pain; my first vivid encounter happened at three years old when a friend of mine closed a heavy metal door on my hand while playing in his house. The door amputated the end of my left hand's middle finger to the bone. If that wasn't traumatic enough, my parents took me to a doctor for a year. This doctor, without anesthesia, would unwrap my bandages every Wednesday and thoughtfully cut open the wound so the flesh would grow underneath the nail, restoring some semblance of a standard finger, albeit missing the very tip. Back then, I couldn't understand the pain, and I suffered greatly, both physically and emotionally. Looking back at that younger version of me, I see the valuable lesson in that experience – I now have a semi-normal-looking finger and, indeed, a much stronger character.

When I was fourteen, doctors also discovered a bone tumor the size of a Silver Eagle coin in the head of my left tibia. First, the doctors warned us that it might be cancerous and that I could potentially lose my leg from the knee downward. After a very painful biopsy, the results came back negative, thank God! But the tumor still needed to be removed. The surgeons developed a new procedure, which involved prolonged surgery. During this operation, I was given too much anesthesia, and I vividly recall finding myself floating in the top corner of the operating room, looking down at my body, and overhearing the surgeons reconstructing my leg after they had extracted the tumor. This experience gave me one of my first metaphysical insights at a young age. It showed me that we are more than our senses can comprehend and that we are spiritual beings with a human experience.

Back in the recovery room, I remember the excruciating pain that wouldn't subside even with the morphine they were administering. I spent four weeks simply lying in bed without being able to move, during the first two weeks of which the pain was relentless. A few days into recovery, I even asked the doctors to amputate my leg so that the pain would end.

Today, I bear the scars, both in my body and in my heart, of these two events. For many years of my life, I felt somewhat incomplete and imperfect from a physical standpoint, almost feeling undeserving of love since I was not normal anymore. But within a year, I learned to use both of my legs. I proved to the world that I was still a champion, winning several rowing competitions in my home country and the US and even becoming the State Champion in my category, where I measured myself with all other crew persons my age in the Midwestern competitions. I had overcome the challenge and learned the difference between pain and suffering on a physical plane. I realized that my body does not define me. We can rise above any physical ailment, including death itself. I know of many who are terminally ill. They find a significant amount of peace before their passing as they accept the finite aspect of life and rejoice in the positive aspects of what they have experienced, except for those who commit suicide who never master the difference between pain and suffering and unfortunately choose to end it all instead of evolving.

In a way, physical pain is somewhat easier to overcome than emotional pain, as the latter tends to linger longer in our hearts. It's often self-induced by the lack of awareness that the universe, or life itself, does not march to the beat of our drum. Instead, events happen for us, not to us, so that we can evolve on our own emotional and spiritual journeys. Emotional and spiritual maturity are optional and only self-realizable with much inner work. Unlike physical maturity, which we all reach by simply aging, how we face life challenges and opportunities determines how well or quickly we attain evolution in these two critical aspects of our being and, essentially, awareness. The key takeaway is that one must accept and surrender to what is to free oneself from the temporary pain caused by the present circumstances and desired life outcomes. In this acceptance, one does not become a renunciant; instead, one embraces the pain, allowing the emotions to permeate the deepest fibers of our being instead of escaping through distraction, addiction, or the compulsory consumption of exogenous things like material goods, experiences, or substances including food, alcohol, or drugs. In the acceptance and the experience of the pain, one must reframe it at our core to symbolize nothing more than guidance for us to become aware of the disconnect between reality and our perceptions. In this reframing of what is, without placing any meaning or connotation on the events that brought the emotional pain, one finds freedom from continuous suffering. I also know a thing or two about emotional suffering; being a natural empath, not only have I experienced overwhelming personal emotional suffering, but I have also felt the suffering of many others around me. It has been through fighting my demons and coping mechanisms that I've learned these lessons, which I am sharing here today so you may also free yourself from self-induced suffering. Pain is not optional; it's a constant of the human condition and quite frankly unavoidable, yet suffering, on the other hand, is always avoidable as it permanently resides in our minds and never outside of us.

Here is the beauty of the tools I am providing you: if you can reframe the pain that you experienced, thus avoiding suffering, you are well on your way to learning a valuable spiritual lesson. We all agreed to come to this earth to experience pain differently and attain the needed growth. Instead of complaining about the curriculum and trying to change the Universe's plan, one can graduate faster by offering less resistance. In surrender, one finds freedom from suffering, realizing that all pain is temporary and, in a way, external to our actions, for the reasons I explained. However, we can avoid suffering ultimately by actively changing our vantage point. By making the sweetest possible lemonade from the lemons that life has brought us, we rise above the physical and emotional planes of existence and master the life lessons brought to us for our benefit.

We become 'jiu-jitsu' masters of life (Jiu-Jitsu - derives from the Japanese "Jū," meaning 'gentle,' and "Jutsu," meaning 'art'; essentially, Jiu-Jitsu is the 'gentle art'). Instead of trying to impose our will upon the world, we simply flow atop the waters of every storm that life brings. The understanding that life happens for us, not to us, provides us with a solid foundation to reframe pain and avoid suffering.

This also provides one of the core foundations for accepting ourselves with all our limitations, which is one step closer to experiencing unconditional love for ourselves and others.

Deciphering Symbols

There is nothing left to chance in Heaven's Plans

This is also factual material for history books, with a few supernatural and non-supernatural events. Still, it's a worthy example for everyone to open their eyes to what is currently being presented on their journeys, as there may be signs already calling your attention that are unknown to you. We all will eventually be called to a higher spiritual communion; I happen to be further to the front of the line where we gain access to the party.

To understand the significance of these events to my life and what I will share, I need to explain some background and their relevance to my destiny. Oscar's wife, my grandmother from my mother's side, was particularly fond of me as I was her first grandchild, and I came to fill the void in her heart that Oscar left after his passing. When I was approximately three or four, I was learning how to speak, and they kept trying to teach me the diminutive of the word grandma, which in Spanish is "abuelita." Since I couldn't enunciate the entire word, I would say "Ita," which is how her new nickname came to be.

So, Ita and I had an extraordinary bond; she was a devoted Catholic and would not only attend mass and pray the rosary but also dedicate her spare time to running the gift shop at the San Martin de Porres Church, consecrated to the Peruvian Saint. Now, with this image of this warm-hearted grandma and my close relationship with her that at many times was significantly better than with my mother, you will see how all the pieces eventually fit together. I was ten years old when Pope John Paul II visited Argentina for the first time in 1982. I remember the commotion of everyone going to see him. During this visit, Ita was honored by receiving a half an inch square Chi-Rho cross blessed by the Pope himself. I don't recall the exact day Grandma entrusted me with it. I should have paid more attention to it or its actual value. Being a teenager, I was frankly focused on other life objectives. Well, Ita requested that I always carry the cross, and if I wasn't going to wear it, I should, at the very least, place it in my wallet as it was small enough. So, I did; she was Ita to me after all.

This cross has been with me ever since, but there was a period during which the cross departed from my side. I want to clarify that I was totally and utterly lost for a significant portion of my life. I never had a vice such as alcohol or drugs, but I certainly lusted and sought pleasure like every average young man with raging testosterone. I had my fair share of trouble and faced the consequences. So, by no means should you think that I've lived the life of a saint. I've been anything but that, and it's essential for me that you know this because I am here for those who don't believe they are redeemable. If you're a devoted Catholic or practice rites through other religions, that is good for you. Keep believing and keep going. I'm also here for you, but this message may not touch you as profoundly because you might already think you know the truth and are most likely so set in your ways that it'll take a miracle for my words to reach you. I am here sharing myself with everyone who is in despair, everyone who is in their darkest of hours. My brothers and sisters need the hope and Truth that my words bring. I am here for all of you who no longer find meaning in the starchy hallways of any religion. Hear me out: I have things to share because I used to be just like you!

There was a period when darkness engulfed me; see, Satan doesn't take lightly the fact that you turned him down. My rejection cost me dearly in every aspect of my life; everything was repeatedly taken from me. I would rebuild, and in one swift move, the forces at play would conspire for me to experience utter misery and betrayal. Lovers, partners, and clients who were asleep and not in communion would be wolves in sheep's clothing and slowly seep into my reality to strike at my weakest. Having lost everything more times than I care to admit to my family and the world, I want you to know that if you choose to embody the Light, you will be tested to the breaking point of all convictions. This journey I am describing is not for the weak of mind, heart, or spirit. You will find yourself on your knees more than you can ever anticipate. However, the beauty of being visited by the Holy Spirit or experiencing some or all the other manifestations, which I will eventually share, certainly makes up for the pain of the journey.

During this bleak time, I underwent a harsh divorce from someone I had been dating, whom I married, to prevent her deportation back to Venezuela. I had never planned to do this, as our relationship wasn't functioning well, but she was financially destitute, and I couldn't abandon her. There had been an instance when I needed someone to vouch for my green card, and this person agreed, under the condition that I pay this kindness forward when possible. I recall vividly awaiting her naturalization and simultaneously hoping for her business to bounce back amidst one of Miami's worst economic downturns when she arrived home, her facial expression revealing despair. She laid down the situation: she had thirty days to marry or face deportation, validating her claim with legal paperwork.

I found myself retreating to the familiar hammock by the water where I had previously talked about Jesus Christ with an individual unknown to me to have a demon within. I spent hours deliberating my dilemma: Do I say No, respecting my emotions, or do I say Yes, upholding my word? Her temperamental nature and our incompatibility were not lost on me. Both choices seemed to lead to losses. Ultimately, I decided to keep my word, though I clarified to her that our relationship wasn't working and we needed to find a solution for our future. True to my commitments, I married her quietly, like a gentleman would.

The next six months saw her at her best until her darkness unfolded, wreaking havoc on my life. I'll skip the detailed narrative, but a significant reference point - the catastrophe culminated with seven police vehicles surrounding my home late on a Saturday night, just before my 41st birthday. I had the foresight to record her last attempt to ensnare me by falsely accusing me of domestic violence to the police that evening. When the police turned up to arrest me, I showed them the video evidence, leading to her arrest instead. After noticing my distress, two empathetic female officers contacted another female Florida State Attorney. She came to my home at three in the morning, enlightened me about my rights, and emphasized that the case was now between the State and this woman; I was a victim of an abusive relationship. She advised me to file for divorce on the following Monday, and so I did, but there's much more to the story.

It was one of my darkest periods; I had given my all, only to end up losing everything. I felt ready to leave the US and contemplated ending it all. Emotionally shattered from the torturous divorce, I was left with a measly $500, unable to afford my mortgage or building expenses, mainly as Miami was in the grips of yet another economic real estate disaster. With no alternatives, I was forced to sell my dream waterfront apartment short, virtually losing everything once again. So why do I reveal these painful experiences, and how do they relate to the narrative of the cross? Without this narrative context, one wouldn't comprehend the depth of darkness I was immersed in and the redemption that came about.

However, when we feel close to surrendering, a helping hand appears, and that of our Heavenly Father extends, especially if we do not renounce him. Though I hadn't explicitly chosen to embody Light rather than Darkness, I was wounded and dispirited. Despite my tireless efforts and the many opportunities I sought, everything seemed stagnant, rapidly collapsing. It was as though every time I came close to achieving a goal, some metaphysical force intervened, snatching it away from me. This may sound subjective and difficult to substantiate, but it's the best way to describe my feelings during that time.

It was in this pit of despair in my life that the following events took place. The cross I carried in my wallet needed to be found after having been misplaced, or that is what I thought. I was so beaten down by life and the prevailing circumstances that I couldn't care less about it. There was one individual whom I will not mention this name, but I will certainly give you a copy of this book one day. When you read it, you will know it is about you! He would invite me to the Emmaus Retreat in South Miami for years. Emmaus Retreat is a spiritual program designed for both men and women, focusing on renewing and strengthening one's relationship with Jesus Christ. But I kept turning him down year after year as I was engulfed in that darkness during and after my divorce. Finally, one day, I answered his call. I had already listed my apartment for sale and accepted my fate, so I figured it was now or never for me to attain peace/enlightenment/redemption. As I was packing what was left of my belongings into a POD, I temporarily moved to a property owned by my family in Broward County. It was the right time to disconnect and try to understand everything. Nobody attending the retreat can openly share what happens, so forgive me if I provide scant details or abstain from sharing to honor this request from organizers.

But I can share what was meaningful and what my intentions were during the retreat. I asked my fellow Emmaus Brothers at my table to pray for my intention: to have our Heavenly Father show me why I was meant to endure such a hard life, why my gifts were not benefiting me but instead a burden, and why I always fell short of the finish line no matter how hard I tried. I demanded an answer before the end of the retreat. Otherwise, I pleaded to be left alone to lead an everyday life. So, we all prayed for that with these exact words and demands. I will walk a thin line next, so please take my word for it, as I can't reveal everything the way it went down to honor the retreat premises and the brothers involved. However, I can say that I was used as an instrument to help someone who had carried a heavy emotional burden in his heart for over twenty years. The Spirit awakened within me, and the right words came forth to alleviate this burden for this extraordinary person at the retreat. The event was so meaningful for this person that he stood up in front of 300 men an hour later and passionately announced it to everyone from the altar facing the congregation. He then pulled out a

Chi-Rho cross about two inches square, mounted on a piece of travertine marble, from his pocket, which he had been carrying for these past twenty years, and pointed to me. I was so embarrassed that I wished the earth would swallow me whole. I did not think much about what I had done, so the last thing I would expect was for someone to call it a "miracle," but this person's best friend rushed from the back of the church to join in the celebration and took to the microphone, beginning to proclaim it as such.

By now, I was ready to get up and leave the room; all eyes were upon me, and I couldn't handle the pressure. The person emotionally healed and moved by these events walked almost angrily toward me. With a stern look in his eyes and nearly yelling at me, he stated, "*I have this message for you,*" and handed me his Chi-Rho cross. The air had turned thick; you could hear a pin drop in the church. I felt as if I were shrinking in my seat. The cross felt like a hot potato to me. Instead of holding on to it, I turned to the guy to my right—seated between me and this gentleman—and passed the cross to him. I planned to stand up and leave. To no avail, the brother, now really annoyed with me, said, "*Read it!!!, read what it says right there.*" So I took back the cross from the guy sitting next to me. To my surprise, I flipped it, and it read, '*I have called you by your name; you are mine.*' Everything calmed down after that. The program for the next two hours was canceled, and everyone was moved. We all left for our respective quarters to do the next assignment, and the retreat continued.

So, why is the cross relevant, and how does this long story lead to teaching? If you need clarification now, imagine me living this as a life journey. By the end of the retreat, two answers were physically provided: one through the cross, which I will revisit shortly, and the second through what eventually became the realization of my destiny. This marked the commencement of my Awakening. As the weeks passed, my own Chi-Rho cross that had somehow disappeared from my wallet mysteriously reappeared. I won't claim the transformation of material objects here; I want to retain some credibility with you. But let's say there is significantly more to this story than I am stating here. Over the years, I came to not only myself and my journey but also the implied meaning in all these symbolisms, the meaning of my name, its etymology, and the fact that when our Heavenly Father chooses you, there is no hiding. You better comply. So, have you ever rejected any experiences? I invite you to summon the courage to seek answers within and from above. There are signs all around us constantly being provided for our growth. We must comply and surrender. Never underestimate the subtlety with which the Ethereal communicates with us in this realm through symbolism, which is meant to point us in the right direction. Open your eyes now!

Our Relationship With Reality

With the world and ourselves

How we show up in and to the world aligns with how we perceive ourselves. It has been my humble experience that we can't change anything everlasting outside ourselves if not by a significant change in how we relate to ourselves. Imagine the world or reality like a big mirror that constantly points us to what is not working in the relationship within ourselves. For those lucky enough to have failed several times, the more complex the blows are, the better; we develop the awareness that a change is needed. Success in every aspect of our existence results from applying a winning formula. Most of the time, these formulas are not written in stone, but the only commonality is that anyone who ever found themselves in a position or place they did not want to be had to change and iterate.

This tedious and often painful process involves confronting the undesired outcome, many of which have negative consequences on every possible aspect of life: physical, psychological, emotional, and even spiritual.

There is an order to life, and in many ways, the same way that there are natural laws governing our physical universe, there are hidden spiritual ones which, once understood, can tilt the balance of the actions we take unto our favor. Humans have been led astray to believe in many societal constructs since their early years, always assuming that our educators and guardians have the best intentions. Unfortunately, it is the case of a transgenerational blind leading people who are blind in the hopes that the next generation can find a better way or not fail in the same painful ways. Every self-made woman or man will tell you that they are a product of their environment and the relationships they kept. Additionally, the sage ones will also be the first to point out that they were lucky enough to find or achieve a healthy relationship with themselves.

Given the importance of these facts, wouldn't it stand to reason that the essential relationship in our present existence, if we are at a crossroads between our present position in life and our desired expectations, is our relationship with our Creator and second to it with ourselves? Wouldn't this even apply to the atheist or agnostic? It does, as, in a sense, you may rightfully believe you are your creator; after all, look, you made yourself to be you throughout your life. Indeed, we must first heal any dysfunctionality within if we expect to show up in the world and have the world show up to us in a different light.

It has been my own arduous and personal experience overtaken seven years ago after being confronted with a hard choice as to how and why my reality was not even close to my anticipated expectations in every desired aspect. Given the distance between the objectives and the current outcomes, I was confronted by the idea that a radical approach was needed if a radical change was expected. As Einstein said, *"The world as we have created it is a process of our thinking. It cannot be changed without changing our thinking."* The same applies to who we are; we can't change it until we change how we perceive ourselves. Within this perception lies the relationship between us and the Divine, whether we want to accept it or not, is indifferent to its existence and how we fit in the overall cosmic tapestry as we are as much of a creation within it and do not exist in a vacuum in relationship to it.

See, it is only by countless trials and error that one attains enlightenment; it is only in the stillness of the silence within that one expands outside. Before becoming truly well-rounded, you must do the inner work; there are no shortcuts. I am tired of watching successful individuals so lopsided in their personas with little to no balance. In pursuing a few of life's material aspects, they neglected the development of other complementary or more meaningful human existential facets such as physical, psychological, emotional, and even spiritual. Yes, they shine bright in their fields of glory; meanwhile, several foundations crumble within them, not allowing for a truly fruitful life. *Our relationships with the world outside of us are valuable, yet the relationship with the world within is invaluable.*

How are you treating yourself lately? Do you truly love who you have become or are becoming? Where are your pain points? What aspects of your persona or personality are you trying consciously or subconsciously to compensate for, and how? I could give countless examples, but I don't believe any list could plausibly be all-encompassing, as there is more than one for each human alive today or that ever lived.

We are little children trying to make sense of the world we live in and how we fit in. No matter our level of success in one field of life, we indeed fail in others. So, one must wonder how, where, and when we must change. Unless we are confronted with defeat, we can't take the trouble to rethink ourselves anew—the reason why there are more business startups during the collapse of an economy than during an expansion. In a never-ending cycle, humans toil to make a living many times, forgetting that all crises are self-inflicted and, to a degree, premeditated. But why do we allow ourselves to become what we have?

One question that always brings my attention to the forefront of my decision-making process is my divine sovereignty, where I have been lied to, and by whom, as my awareness expands in a world that is broken in many ways. Our societies are all at a breaking point, our Divine rights threatened by evermore draconian government overreach. I question myself: how much should we tolerate our freedoms curtailed in the name of a fictitious system that only keeps benefiting a few? At the same time, the great majority have no say. How are these constructs even plausible? As there is a correlation between how we treat ourselves and others the same way by reciprocity, there must be a correlation between how we allow others to be treated.

You probably wonder how this is related to our relationships and, most importantly, our relationship with ourselves. It is so apparent that it is almost painful for me to point it out. We would never sit still and allow ourselves to be mistreated by the world around us if we did not allow ourselves to mistreat ourselves in the first place. Unless we hold ourselves in high regard and our self-worth is intact with the conscious understanding that we are sobering Divine beings having a human experience, we would not allow any negative self-talk; we would constantly iterate our belief system until we overcome societal norms and eradicate all falsehoods from our essence.

Only by living a righteous life encompassing the totality of our existence can we honor ourselves and those around us. No human should, in a sound mind, accept anything less than fair treatment, not only by themselves but also by the world around them and the society they belong to.

But then again, how could we all expect to live in a prosperous society where the unrighteous are given free rein to dictate the rest of the laws?

I could not comprehend the degree to which our world is genuinely broken until I was made aware of how much I was broken. Once I realized that the only way to take control of the unwelcome outcomes was to, in essence, take control of myself and systematically work on uncovering what aspects within me were hidden from myself, which were not working, I was not able to change the world around me.

Within these aspects, at the core, was my relationship with our Heavenly Father and Creator. Only when I surrendered to the unknowns in these regards did my heart and life start flourishing in a well-rounded manner. I can attest that no poorer individual attains wealth at the price of integrity. I have already covered the power of words and thoughts in a prior letter, so for those who read it, it is easy to jump to the conclusion that we all are the products of our thoughts and words and how we honor these words; it is also how we show up in the world.

Cheating and stealing seem to be the norm today in every regard, but those victories are short-lived, and everyone who thinks that business is still a zero-sum game has much to learn from life itself and the actual fabric of what the world is.

Honor yourself within yourself, allow for the seed of self-love to start germinating, and allow yourself to be you. For every limiting factor, cherish it as an opportunity for self-discovery. Push the boundaries within to conquer the change you seek outside yourself. Iteration is the mother of perfection; success is the mirror of defeat; one can't exist without the other, as all duality is a game for us to find ourselves within.

The answer is always the same: unconditional love for oneself and others.

Reciprocity of Shadows

The Persistent Mystery of The Ever-Present Magic

By now, we have already tacitly implied that my life has been anything but an everyday affair. Albeit all efforts were made to try to slip into the shadows of existence and remain within the commonality of mundane life, the unexpected continued showing up. The longer I would turn my attention away from the inexplicable events calling my attention to a conscious communion with the Divine Forces at play, the harder the knocking on the doors of my life would become. Right after the events I related to in a prior chapter, right past my forty-first birthday, my real awakening began, which I would like to point to. In those days, I had placed my condo for sale and awaited a complete departure from South Beach. I enjoyed running five miles from my home to South Pointe Park and back every other day. One day in April, I wasn't feeling inclined as my depression had kicked in due to the severity of the divorce and the lack of financial resources. So, I decided to ride my nice BMW motorcycle to the beach instead and parked by the SLS Hotel at the end of 17th Street. When I arrived, I noticed two ladies doing a photoshoot, one of whom was in a bikini and the other being the photographer. Right as I was walking away, one approached me and asked if they could use my motorcycle as a prop for their pictures, to which I agreed and left them to their affairs while I went for a walk on the sand by the ocean.

Having just recently been able to free myself from the most pervasive of emotionally abusive relationships I had ever endured, the last priority in my mind was to establish another romantic relationship with a woman. I needed to find my bearings and heal, to somehow pull through the misery of the circumstances and prevail. Hence, I did not even think about flirting, let alone establishing a conversation, but it's funny: the less you seek, the more things tend to find you. After my three-mile walk, to my astonishment, both ladies were patiently waiting for me upon my return. The model who was the subject of the pictures came towards me and said, "*I have been waiting for you for over an hour; here is my card. Please call me; I have something to tell you.*" I looked at her with total disdain as I noticed that she was also from Venezuela due to her accent, and my ex-wife, who was making my life a living hell at that time, was also Venezuelan. So, my broken life, heart, and spirit were almost having an allergic reaction. I stood still; I did not know what to answer. My awareness was called to a huge scar, which I had not noticed on her until now. I won't delve into the details, but I realized that the person who was in front of me had undergone an excruciating surgery of sorts, and my empathy kicked in. I thanked her for the card, told her I would consider it, and rode my motorcycle away. The irony is that at that moment, this woman was sent to return to me what the other had taken away: my self-worth. But what are the odds of choosing two similar tools to do the exact opposite of one another? It was a sign I would later understand as my integration into higher planes of existence occurred.

A month had passed, and I had not called her yet. Her business card sat there on my desk. While I overlooked the bay's water, I pondered my life situation while desperately working on real estate deals to solve my financial and divorce situations. I just wanted everything to be over to sell my belongings and go backpacking. At that point, I couldn't care less about remaining within the confines of my life. But one morning, when nothing else was happening, something within me made me stare at her card for a long time. I finally picked up the phone and called her. She knew who I was and told me she had been expecting my call all this time, and I must see her immediately. I mentioned that I was going through a rough patch and could only invite her for coffee. She responded that she knew more about me than I could imagine and was inviting me. We agreed to meet at 3:00 pm at Books & Books in Coral Gables.

As I arrived at our appointment, I was greeted by the cafe owner, who brought just about everything on the menu. This was the second banquet to which I had been treated in the past thirty days, somehow without me asking for it, in my honor. The prior one happened through another dear spiritual friend living in Vegas at the time, and I went to visit right after the ordeal during my birthday the previous month. Anyhow, I digress, but I want you to understand that the Divine will somehow work things out in your favor once you come on board, no matter how hard the circumstances may get. Remember that the king of this world is not the King in Heaven, and your life will undoubtedly become shambles more than once.

Moving on, this lady proceeded to greet me, requested that I eat something first, and then asked me to pay close attention to what she was about to tell me with an open mind. I won't go into all the details as they are irrelevant, but like the bodybuilder event, she told me that God had spoken that day in front of the SLS Hotel. She received what I like to call now a "download," which involves transferring a certain amount of awareness to the forefront of our consciousness, both in terms of information and applied knowledge pertinent to the circumstances we are experiencing. It always comes from Divine precedence, and during her encounter, our Heavenly Father requested that she share a large amount of information about me that was not publicly available online and pertinent to my life's journey so she could establish credibility with me. After establishing this credibility, she delivered the following message: *"Tell him that I am very upset for him being so ungrateful for everything I have given him and that I am expecting him to return to me."* Remember this, as it is one of the keys to accessing the Kingdom we have been told about for the past 2,000 years. If you want the ability to conjure the miraculous, it all starts by being grateful even for the worst circumstances. A true Master understands that everything is an illusion and our natural state of being is One with the Divine. No matter what we experience, gratitude for the lesson or the opportunity ahead is the key to watering the garden and creating an oasis in the middle of the desert.

Back to that day, I didn't know what my face looked like as I was eating and almost choked. Indeed, I was upset with God. After having chosen to embody Light and turned away from every single one of my life's material aspirations while doing good for others, I found myself in the current predicament. Little did I know then or understand the fabric of life and its purpose or how the Universe conspires for our benefit and growth. Again, we can't attain any lasting gifts if not by self-realization of what we seek outside of us within. As such, I couldn't comprehend then that God was granting these and many other opportunities for my growth while keeping a watchful eye on me in the playground of life. His allowance of dire circumstances was not an oversight but intended, so I would willingly renounce my ego aspirations and turn my focus to my spiritual journey. Being extremely stubborn then, I was determined to remain self-sufficient, severed from the Divine Bounty waiting for me if I would just let go. All the signs were there, pointing to the necessary clues of the teaching, but over eleven years ago, I was still utterly asleep at the helm of my life. Little did I understand the concepts I have shared throughout this book, and frankly, being of service to everyone who my words reach is the driving force of this enormous endeavor to share the greatness of the Spirit that resides within each one of us. If we allow ourselves to live in communion with our Heavenly Father, our life takes an entirely different meaning and path. A path certainly less traveled but one full of abundance and enriching circumstances.

Regarding messengers, now we must jump forward in the timeline approximately six to seven years and skip other events for now. However, in this chapter, I want to share a continuation of how the Divine will send messengers for us to connect back. So, I had gone through my dark night of the soul during which I experienced the most painful of emotional losses; then, I had lost the love of my life and her three children. I was recomposing my life, and to heal, I went on a dating app, which was an adventure of its own. I could write a whole book about the perils of men in online dating and Southeast Florida, but I will keep it family-friendly here. During one of these dates, I met a very interesting petite woman from a family of Mexican descent. We had an incredible connection, and I was extremely drawn to her in more ways than one; I sensed we had unbelievable chemistry, but by then, I had begun my awakening, and my integrity would not allow me to embark on a relationship if from the onset there was a red flag or something which called me away from my chosen lifestyle.

Additionally, I wasn't open to meaningless exchanges and desired to find true connections. So, after only one date, I turned her down the following week after careful introspection. Let's say she was upset with my transparency and honest reasons, and she hung up the phone. Months had gone by, when one afternoon, my phone kept ringing off the hook one a Friday while I was on another call. Of course, I was on a business conference call, so that I couldn't pick up, but the unknown number was relentless. At one point, I got an SMS stating, *"Please pick up, it is me... so sorry I have been a bitch to you; I have something of extreme importance to tell you"*. I responded, *"Sorry, I am on a call. I will get back to you shortly,"* which I did. When I called, she told me that the day before, while attending a mass in her church and during the reading of a passage from the New Testament Book by my patron, St. James, God spoke to her and told her to call me immediately and that I should come with her and her whole family to mass on Sunday. She had to summon the courage to call me for the past 24 hours because she didn't even know if I would believe her. As you know, these occurrences were not uncommon in my life, so I put her at ease, letting her know that such events had happened already, and I was happy to comply.

Sunday came, and there I was, sitting next to her and all her family at a church north of the Fort Lauderdale Airport of a denomination I had never heard of before. Again, I stopped going to church long ago, as after all the apparitions, revelations, and direct one-on-one interactions with the Holy Spirit and our Heavenly Father, there was nothing else I needed there. During the mass, the pastor read two passages that were almost direct answers to existential life questions I had at that time. When I thought everything that I had come to receive was provided, I proceeded to say goodbye and prepared to leave the church. To my disbelief, she said, "*Wait, don't go. You still haven't received what you came here for*". She pointed to an older woman waiting at the side of our area, instructed me to sit by this lady's side, and said she had a message for me. Curious as always about the supernatural, I decided to comply. I won't provide many details because what was revealed to me that morning was a prophecy of what would come to pass over the following years, along with what is already passing and will still come for me. The Spirit channeled through this woman knew intimate details of my life that not even my parents could have guessed. To establish credibility, it ensured I was paying attention and took the matter seriously. By the end of the channel, I was sobbing uncontrollably, both tears of joy and of acknowledgment that I wasn't going crazy and that indeed my whole life's journey had a greater purpose than what my little mind could understand then and there. So once again, Spirit was showing me the way through the storms of life, and all I needed to do was to let go and surrender, be grateful for every circumstance, and keep showing up and allowing with blind conviction to be guided by it through my every next step.

The whole point of this chapter is to shed light on the help awaiting us if we turn away from our ways and allow ourselves to be guided. You need a noble, open, loving heart to overcome the lower levels of awareness and enter higher levels of understanding. You may not perceive perfection within the circumstances at this very moment, but then again, this is exactly the point in life's journey design. Let go, allow, and flow!

I Am What I Am

The Power of Words

What if a superpower that held one of the keys to existence was hidden in both women and men? Our thoughts dictate our existence in more ways than we can comprehend. Essentially, we become what we think. The early records of many scriptures highlight the relevance and importance of the spoken word, which always follows a prior thought. Very few among us have had the opportunity to elevate our consciousness and become aware of the ongoing noise in our heads. That small voice within constantly reminds us of what is or isn't.

What if we could raise our conscious awareness above the autopilot neuronal thought patterns? Much like a fish in water, unaware at times that it's swimming, we could lift ourselves above the relentless self-talk. I remember vividly the day this breakthrough occurred to me over a decade and a half ago. I had just finished reading 'The Power of Now' by Eckhart Tolle. I was sitting in Maurice Gibb Memorial Park in South Beach, overlooking the bay in the late afternoon. The golden sun sparkled on the small waves of the bay. A gentle spring breeze surrounded me as I allowed myself to appreciate the beauty and forget, for a moment, all the painful instances of my existence. To many, including myself, my life was a rat race full of unbearable inadequacies. This revelation happened almost instantaneously, which I attribute to an act of Grace. For the first time in my life, the little voice in my head fell silent, and I peered into the true nature of reality. My senses expanded beyond the normal, and the mesmerizing beauty of the world around me completely captivated me for what seemed like an eternity. It was a preview of what would come over the next decade and a half. The experience of our natural state of being, which some describe as "Oneness," is indescribable yet genuinely transformative.

That day, I realized in a gnostic way that there was much more to our existence than I can still comprehend, but that my self-talk, positively or negatively, had much to do with the reality I experienced. An interesting empirical fact in my journey has been that receiving Grace is unlike a replicable science experiment. You can do the same practices repeatedly and attain different results; hence, any practices, rituals, or prayers may yield completely different outcomes even for the same practitioner. However, one of the critical aspects is that one must always be open and a seeker until one finds the Divine within. Once found, one must stop seeking and melt into the fiber of existence, as this is the ultimate spiritual act.

The acceptance of reality itself is, in fact, the highest manifestation of spiritual mastery.

In the meantime, one must navigate the complex weave of our relationship with reality and the implications of our positive or negative self-talk, fears, and traumas. Each provides a canvas for us to self-define in front of the experiences themselves. Will we rise to the opportunity life gives us, or will we succumb to the miseries it instills upon us? One may erroneously think that financial abundance would take away most of our life pains. Yet, I tell you, having experienced both ends of the spectrum in these regards, financial abundance is but a mild anesthetic that robs us of the opportunity to fully embrace the forces within us to embody our highest potential. In other words, I know first-hand that my greatest triumphs have come through the embrace of lack and pain, not the soothing of exuberance. Our character and relationship with Divinity are more accessible when no material distractions exist. The ultimate Truth can only be known to those who find it in the void within. We can't make the time or space to discover the world within unless we are deprived of the outside world. No one can do this for you; one alone must embark on this journey; there are no mentors, masters, gurus, or scriptures that can transfer this wisdom; at best, they can point to the knowledge attained through their journeys. Wisdom is, in fact, a gnostic experience and, in many cases, the result of Grace and our Father's mercy upon each one of us. All that anyone can do is point you in the right direction, but the road is narrow and full of never-ending steep inclines.

So, how does all of this relate to the power of words and our thoughts behind them? There is a direct correlation between what we state or believe to be and what we perceive to be. The truth is indeed in the eye of the beholder. One can easily perceive an entirely different truth than our neighbor, and both are correct. In other words, all reality and truth perceived through our senses are subjective. The only absolute truth I could find in my existence has been the Divine itself, yet even this can barely be comprehended in a minuscule aspect by any human mind. All the science I have studied has presented exceptions within the observations. That is all that science is a mathematical description of observations within specific parameters and accepted definitions, and in essence, it is still subjective. Yet you speak with scientists with such a mental stronghold due to the indoctrination received during their education that it takes only a few great ones to accept how little they genuinely know; the same goes for many other professions, like doctors, engineers, etc.

It takes a lot of humility and courage to go against the societal norm, think beyond what we have believed to be "true," and realize that everything is, in fact, subjective and seen through the lens of our senses and preconditioned minds. And what is behind all of this? The words we use. Reality or its definition is constructed in our minds using words. There is no more powerful combination than the words *"I am..."* Within them is the lock and key of our self-identifications; entire civilizations have flourished or were doomed due to their self-identifications. Every single most atrociously devastating act of humanity, including wars, has been done due to the subjective identification of "I am... followed by an adjective". Yet the truth is that at our core, there is nothing but emptiness; in that emptiness, one can find Divinity. But unless we gather the courage to completely disidentify ourselves with what "we believe to be real," we can never find it.

The only reason Jesus stated to let the children come to me, "because theirs is the Kingdom of Heaven," was because a small child still has not self-identified with anything. In such innocence, they can still coexist within the natural communion with our Father or, as others call it, The Holy Spirit. One must empty oneself to be in its presence. Realizing this, one can rebuild oneself to embody either darkness or light. Through a conscious choice, we are granted our free will to experience reality, which is always subjective based on the eye of the beholder, as even death itself is a mere rite of passage and can be seen as the end of the beginning.

My question to you today is, if you had a superpower that could alter the fabric of space and time itself and, like a tiny seed, could be planted in your subconscious mind and eventually provide a juicy, sweet fruit, would you use it properly, or would you squander it?

I invite you today to do an exercise; if you accept the challenge of changing your identifications, why not choose the ones that would make you a better version of yourself? A version that the whole world would turn around and look at you for inspiration? Here is a list of valuable self-identifications; you can read it every morning when you wake up as an inspiration for how you want to show up in the world today. And who knows, maybe if you put in the work, you will eventually find yourself bringing exactly what you state you are to the rest of the world.

Creating a comprehensive list of all positive human attributes would be extensive, but we can start you off with this substantial list. Remember, this list might not cover every positive attribute, as the concept of positivity can vary significantly across cultures, perspectives, and contexts. Here's a good beginning:

I am beautiful, I am lovable, I am perfect, I am harmonious, I am intelligent, I am kind, I am compassionate, I am strong, I am resilient, I am confident, I am brave, I am creative, I am imaginative, I am thoughtful, I am generous, I am understanding, I am patient, I am diligent, I am dedicated, I am honest, I am trustworthy, I am respectful, I am optimistic, I am hopeful, I am grateful, I am joyful, I am enthusiastic, I am adaptable, I am flexible, I am resourceful, I am persistent, I am courageous, I am adventurous, I am ambitious, I am curious, I am open-minded, I am empathetic, I am supportive, I am dependable, I am loyal, I am friendly, I am sociable, I am considerate, I am polite, I am refined, I am elegant, I am articulate, I am wise, I am insightful, I am reflective, I am serene, I am peaceful, I am calm, I am soothing, I am reassuring, I am protective, I am nurturing, I am healing, I am spiritual, I am faithful, I am devoted, I am passionate, I am energetic, I am vibrant, I am lively, I am playful, I am fun, I am humorous, I am light-hearted, I am cheerful, I am positive, I am inspiring, I am motivated, I am influential, I am empowering, I am leading, I am pioneering, I am innovative, I am progressive, I am visionary, I am altruistic, I am humanitarian, I am philanthropic, I am benevolent, I am caring, I am forgiving, I am accepting, I am inclusive, I am diverse, I am eclectic, I am unique, I am original, I am authentic, I am genuine, I am sincere, I am modest, I am humble, I am unpretentious, I am unassuming, I am mindful, I am aware, I am conscious, I am enlightened, I am awakened, I am liberated, I am free, I am secure, I am safe, I am protected, I am prosperous, I am successful, I am affluent, I am wealthy, I am healthy, I am well, I am fit, I am strong-minded, I am balanced, I am stable, I am centered, I am harmonized, I am synchronized, I am aligned, I am coherent, I am congruent, I am consistent, I am orderly, I am systematic, I am methodical, I am efficient, I am effective, I am proficient, I am skilled, I am talented, I am gifted, I am extraordinary, I am remarkable, I am exceptional, I am outstanding, I am excellent, I am superb, I am splendid, I am magnificent, I am majestic, I am grand, I am impressive, I am striking, I am stunning, I am dazzling, I am shining, I am glowing, I am radiant, I am bright, I am luminous, I am vivid, I am colorful, I am vibrant, I am rich, I am deep, I am pure, I am clear, I am transparent, I am lucid, I am limpid, I am sparkling, I am shimmering, I am twinkling, I am gleaming, I am glistening, I am glittering, I am scintillating, I am brilliant, I am genius, I am sage, I am philosopher, I am guru, I am master, I am expert, I am authority, I am leader, I am chief, I am head, I am principal, I am guide, I am mentor, I am coach, I am instructor, I am teacher, I am educator, I am scholar, I am academic, I am literate, I am knowledgeable, I am learned, I am erudite, I am intellectual, I am brainy, I am clever, I am smart, I am quick-witted, I am witty, I am sharp, I am keen, I am acute, I am sagacious, I am perceptive, I am discerning, I am judicious, I am prudent, I am wise, I am sapient, I am sage, I am enlightened, I am illuminated, I am radiant, I am shining, I am brilliant, I am glowing, I am incandescent, I am effulgent, I am resplendent, I am splendid, I am magnificent, I am glorious, I am sublime, I am exalted, I am elevated, I am uplifted, I am blessed, I am that I am, I am unconditional love.

Divine Encounters

Embark on a Journey of Supernatural Realizations of Purpose

If you have read this far in the book, then you are ready for me to reveal the last but most profound manifestations. These revelations have transformed me from the man I once was to the one I've become. Over the past two years, I have allowed myself to be guided and comply with the natural order of life on this earth. This journey, aligned with how nature or the Divine intended us to live, has led me to a diet and lifestyle devoid of manufactured products, cooked animal flesh, derived products, and anything frozen. Combined with fasting practices and meditation, I sporadically attain heightened states of consciousness. This event tends to happen in the early hours between 3:00 am and 5:00 am when I get up and sit in total stillness. In that stillness, I allow myself to go inward. Most of the time, there is no answer to my stillness, but I remain grateful and move on to my normal daily activities. But occasionally, a telepathic download occurs with inspiration for the tasks at hand or the answers to prevailing questions. I won't disclose the totality of the experiences in this book because it is not about my journey but the opportunity for you to embark on yours and what you may expect from it. I will add that there were two events on one day. I awakened early in the morning and wasn't rested enough to get up; something implausible and improbable happened. All the lights in my house were turned on by themselves, and I understood the message and got up to meditate that day.

Now, I would like to share the three times that I was awakened in such a manner between July and December 2022. During these times, I was complying with the hardest of tests of surrendering and letting go of everyone to whom I was still emotionally attached in this lifetime. I don't want to provide further details, but you must know there is a point in your spiritual evolution when you must let go of every loving relationship you are attached to. It is like a rite of passage to one of the levels; it is not that there will not be other loving relationships after that, but it is a test of what you love more. Either you love our Father in Heaven more, or you love your current life more. Nothing will be taken from you, but you are invited and allowed to let go consciously. This process is almost like dying without physical death. It is the renunciation of the complete identity of whom you had become until that day to make room for your Truth to permeate your being in the future. This level of Spiritual Mastery is not easy, so I was greeted with three unique visits in the early morning. This time, the messenger had to give me audible and visual evidence that these opportunities were being presented to ensure I was ready. To ensure that it was not something I was making up.

There I was, probably at 4:00 am on a Wednesday in mid-July; I woke up to a spotlight illuminating me from above my head while the rest of the room was in complete darkness. In other words, this light was not coming from a light bulb in any of the lamps in my room. In complete awe, I looked around me and at my arms and hands, and yes, this was happening. Something above me was shining. I briefly tried to look up to ascertain what it was, but it was so bright that it was blinding. Immediately, as my awareness of the event began to percolate in my mind, I felt an overwhelming presence that entered my being and gave me an incredible sense of peace. Then, the voice that had visited when I was six, which I mentioned at the beginning of this book, spoke.

Meanwhile, white sparkles of light flashed throughout my field of view as the words were spoken. I won't delve into all the details of the life circumstances I was enduring then, but again, I was victim to darkness in all my business endeavors, and two wolves in sheep's clothing had already entered my life, preparing once again to steal everything I had. The Holy Spirit simply made one request of me: *"Become nothing once again with me..."* In layperson's terms, this means surrender, letting go of my toiling, and allowing our Heavenly Father to take the reins of my life and let go of expectations and desired outcomes. Throughout this book, I have been intimating to take a passenger seat in your own life and let God dictate a greater purpose, one that our tiny minds can't even begin to visualize. I did precisely that, and in the following months, things worked out to allow me to go unscathed. Unfortunately, darkness is also relentless, and although I had prevailed and won, it came back with a vengeance the very next year at the hands of the same two individuals.

As life progressed toward the end of 2022, I was already in complete surrender, accepting the act of letting go of those dear to my heart and understanding that I needed to take on what was coming next in my journey. To attain a higher level of awareness, I proceeded during the first two weeks of December to undertake a fast, only supplying my body with fresh squeezed fruit juice for this period and focusing on early morning meditations. Every Friday until the following Sunday morning, I followed Jesus Christ's teachings of water fast, detailed in the long-suppressed Gnostic Gospels found in the desert in Egypt in the mid-1940s. In these teachings, you will learn about a Jewish congregation that lived a completely different lifestyle back then; they were essentially vegetarians and would attain supernatural healing powers as they communed with Nature and the Divine in a Gnostic way, meaning, without needing third-party intermediation.

So, it happened twice again in each instance that I fasted. Each Sunday at 4:00 am, I was awakened again by the blinding spotlight over my head and the Holy Spirit, who provided detailed instructions on my questions about my life and the next steps. I will not provide you with the details as they are very personal to my journey and unimportant to yours. However, this short but pivotal section's key takeaway is that the supernatural awaits communion once you cleanse yourself of man-made filters and blocks. The human body is like an antenna; you can tune it to lower frequencies or access higher ones depending on what you put into it. I have experienced everything I share here by experimenting with these aspects myself. Suppose I eat animal-based, cooked, or frozen products. In that case, my level of awareness decreases, and I experience what I like to call a disconnect from these higher realms, which are always present, providing insights and guidance. There is no obligation to live a different life; we do have free will, after all. But I made the resolve to take advantage of everything I can experience in this reality as it is part of my Soul's journey. Shouldn't you do the same, or at least ask the questions that lead to your revelations?

Reflections of the Self

How Our Judgements of Others Reflect Back on Us

A grand game of hide-and-seek is going on. What we judge others on is the root of duality in our existence and, in a way, is pointing the way to our self-healing, as we can only recognize what we know to be true within ourselves in others. There is only one antidote and shortcut to escape this relentless game, which, although you may think you can temporarily win by avoiding situations, will eventually come back to haunt you with a vengeance. Unconditional love and acceptance halt the simulation and are the master keys to unlocking the lesson and progressing to the next one.

I am giving you the lesson's conclusion at the beginning of the passage, but I know that many, if not all, will not grasp its meaning, as it takes effort and introspection to unlock this wisdom. Again, I provide knowledge based on my understanding, which is the gnostic realization of knowledge.

I can't impart wisdom; you must seek it on your own. As I always state, you must perform the inner work of introspection, forgiveness, seeking, aligning with the Truth, and opting to embody Light, not darkness. Remember, there is no absolute right or wrong; it is what we determine within our scale of values. Now, you might argue that this assertion is incorrect and that behaviors like genocide, suicide, murder, violence, rape, etc., are all wrong. Indeed, on my scale of values and wisdom, I find no value in any of the mentioned situations. Yet, from a gnostic perspective, knowing that we are indestructible and our consciousness moves on to other realms after our death, I can understand why some souls might need to experience said conditions to learn firsthand, not to embody these energies again. Once you learn to love unconditionally, you realize the magic and great gift behind each life and the sanctity of the Spirit inhabiting each being. I never speak to the other person's ego from my heart when conducting in-person interventions. I always reach out to the part of me trapped in the individual in front of me, as I know that we are all One in Spirit and that there is no "other" than me within everyone else. This approach allows me to quickly transfer the spiritual lesson I've already attained through my journey and distill it into wisdom, much like two resonating tuning forks.

In other words, by utilizing the shortcuts of the simulation that I've already mastered on prior levels, I can easily reach into the core of the being in front of me and heal the SAVI residing within them. As I have already done the work, it's child's play to bestow the magic and be the cure for others. The more I develop myself, the more layers I unlock within my reality, and the more I can serve others. The more I freely give of myself, the more I receive back from the Universe in an ever-expanding cycle contrary to the law of entropy in physics. Indeed, in this case, the Universe is moving from a lower state of energy and disorder to a higher level of energy and Divine Order. Go figure that one out, scientist. There is always an exception to all your postulates; sorry, I couldn't resist myself as I giggled while writing this sentence. All I know is that I don't know anything, and with this humility, I share my observations with you all.

So, you may ask how you can work on yourself and improve and what the first step on this introspective path is. Reality is constantly beckoning you to embark on this journey, but we need to be more relaxed and focused on our lives, whether purposely or not. We are surrounded by distractions like cellphones, TVs, computers, stimulants, alcohol, drugs, sex, etc., even to begin to confront reality for what it is. One must perform a hard reset and create the space for contemplation. I do not necessarily recommend any spiritual practices, as once you know the Truth, you realize that they are not ends in themselves but a means to an end and that the essence of who you are is immutable from the beginning of time. As I've been explaining, you can also pray all you want to a God outside of you, but that also can be in vain as the Truth is waiting for you inside you. Once you awaken to your True Identity, there is no need for any spiritual practice, prayer, or religion. There is only the choice of being in Communion with our essence — our union between our Soul or Spirit with our Heavenly Father — or falling back to sleep in the slumber of the 3D simulation. This is the most accurate way I found to describe it. Our choices concerning the food we eat, the drinks we consume, and the space we hold can open or close the portal within us for this awakening communion. Now, I'll be the first to admit that I have had extensive periods of this Communion, also known as enlightenment, during which the majority, if not all, of the revelations in my written passages have come. However, let me reiterate that there is NOTHING special about me and what is within me, and these states of heightened consciousness are attainable by every human being who ever walked this earth. I've been fortunate to have suffered enough to be left with no choice but to do the inner work. Knowing what I am, I must share this with everyone willing to listen because it is the next step in my spiritual evolution. Serving others is serving myself; loving everyone unconditionally with no judgment is loving myself and appreciating every aspect I observe in others.

The power for construction or destruction exists within humanity, and we can co-create or co-destroy. We can serve the Light or the darkness. Including me, I could wake up one day disconnected from my higher self and become judgmental and emotional. Generally, these days, which occur more sparsely now than before, are the beacon of Light drawing my attention to unresolved wounds or areas in myself that need work and unconditional love. This leads me to the key I have been trying to share so far. Everything you see outside of you in the mirror of your brother or sister standing across from you reflects facets of your being that need integration. Whatever still triggers you in your daily interactions is the resistance within, pointing you towards aspects of yourself that you must confront.

Once you can be non-judgmental, it signals that you have finalized the work related to that aspect within yourself. You will understand that whatever is happening for the others before you is perfect and complete in their spiritual journey and that the simulation allows them to address themselves. You can choose to be a silent observer, allowing them to experience what they must, or if you notice that they are kind-hearted and ready to overcome their blind spots, you could intervene and share your spiritual wisdom, helping them evolve to your level of awareness. Refrain from thinking that this is not an iterative game; once you have gained understanding, you must demonstrate your mastery of the Universe by tackling the lessons head-on in your journey. You will be tested on the gifts revealed until you truly become a Sensei, a term for a teacher or instructor, typically in Japanese martial arts. It means *"a person born before another"* or "one who comes before." This is the key to understanding that we are all One, overcoming similar spiritual lessons in our ascension to become One with our Heavenly Father. This is the missing key in all religions, one that they never disclose because they aim to control rather than empower you. Conversely, I am here to guide you to the relativity of everything you once believed to be accurate and share my journey to the ultimate Truth.

Throughout my recent development stages, I have repeatedly sought to understand the ultimate Truth. As I've already explained, over two hundred days before this writing, I was given quite the answer one random day at noon while in the Ionian Sea. For what seemed like all of eternity, condensed into a few minutes, I experienced the complete Communion of my consciousness with that of our Heavenly Father. I was shown gnostically what Jesus Christ came to share with us over 2,000 years ago. Much of the awareness revealed during this Communion is for my knowledge only regarding my journey. However, I can attest that everyone reading this can attain the same if they genuinely embark on the Journey Within! As the veil began to lift between the Ethereal realms and my reality, the explorer and adventurer in me couldn't resist but embark on the ultimate adventure. Although the material aspects of life are always appealing, they are merely temporary, even more so than us. I decided that I would make this lifetime count, and if I was put on this earth for a purpose greater than my professional titles and career, it was time for me to must up the courage to explore the full potential of this purpose. Hence, the writings typically come to me after a 24-hour fast between 3:30 am and 5:00 am, which are the hours when the content flows from me to the paper without even having to focus on a single thought. This lesson has been pressing me for the past 48 hours as snippets of awareness come to me daily. This morning, I was awoken at 3:35 am and decided that if I was to have any peace, I needed to start writing what was trying to come through me.

So, reverting to where we started, if you judge a situation or someone, you will encounter this repeatedly until you finally understand that what you are judging and resisting is an unresolved aspect within yourself. Either you realize you have the potential to commit the same act or circumstance, or you can't reconcile it with your notions of right and wrong. You can't love others or yourself unconditionally if you maintain any prejudices. The labels you create to guide your ego through life are all fictitious; the truth is that nothing exists outside of your labels. Unfortunately, we are taught to attach labels to everything from birth, which is how we are shaped and made to conform to society. In our education, we are encouraged to fit into even narrower bands of identity to serve the industrialized world according to the Prussian educational system.

The Prussian education system refers to the system established in Prussia due to the educational reforms in the late 18th and early 19th centuries, which has had a widespread influence since then. The Prussian education system was introduced as a fundamental concept in the late 18th century and was significantly expanded after Prussia's defeat at the early stages of the Napoleonic Wars.

The Prussian educational reforms inspired similar changes in other countries and remain crucial to understanding contemporary nation-building projects and their consequences. The Prussian education system's emphasis on obedience, rigid class-based stratification, centralized control with standardized curricula, and narrow focus on industrialization have been criticized as significant shortcomings that persist in modern education systems influenced by this model. These flaws have raised concerns about stifling creativity, perpetuating socioeconomic disparities, limiting local autonomy and innovation, and failing to adequately prepare students for the demands of a knowledge-based economy that requires critical thinking, adaptability, and a broader range of skills beyond technical training. This is why I am taking the time to shed light on these matters, elevate our awareness, and assist you in reaching a higher state of consciousness. It will enable the right decision-makers to question the "*normal,*" the systems, and themselves to find alternative means to run society. We are achieving better than we once were. Unfortunately, what worked yesterday does not work today, and it's time we all awaken and shift our perceptions instead of inflicting the same damage on each other generation after generation.

All my writings don't imply an answer; they highlight flaws in our rationality, our interaction with reality, and ourselves and others. We can't force anything on anyone; we are not meant to be the ones dictating how to save the world, as the world doesn't need saving. We can be catalysts for change within ourselves and start embodying the Light once we find it. By tirelessly shining this Light within us, we can instill better ways of interacting, socializing, gathering, and achieving in humanity. But we must lift our heads from the daily chores and concentrate on finding this Light within us to reach our maximum potential within our lifetimes. Evolution and change are intrinsic to our reality, and resisting is futile.

We either grow and adapt to what the environment demands or perish; collectively, we have served our purpose and are no longer needed. Nature is perfect in many ways that might be considered brutal by human standards; however, we can learn a lot by observing how other animal species interact within themselves and the environment.

We're not above Nature, and even if we create our concrete jungles, we can't escape the inherent realities encoded in our DNAs and how these survival mechanisms dictate our behaviors. We can only harness opportunities that might otherwise go unnoticed in our constant quest for survival by attaining higher awareness and presence of mind.

This passage has a lot to digest, but again, all these points come through me as I write to draw your attention to aspects of your existence that you have yet to delve deeper into. Whatever you resisted in this writing points to an opportunity for you to look within and ascertain why and what is bothering you. That may be the whole point of this exercise: to help you question yourself, your beliefs, and what you have been taught during your entire life is accurate, but it isn't the only way to approach things.

Please find time for introspection away from distractions and cultivate a habit of seeking silence in your busy life, in which you disconnect and start journeying within yourself to find the answers to everything happening outside of you. And once you start seeing everything for what it truly is, it becomes easy. Remember what I initially stated: the only solution is acceptance and unconditional love if you aim to overcome the simulation level. There isn't anything to impose on others; you only need to love yourself, and the rest will flow naturally, as we are all but One.

Spiritual Lesson Summary

Chapters Key Points

A Call to Be

Together, these teachings emphasize the importance of self-acceptance, understanding our inner observer, recognizing our interconnectedness, and embracing the journey of self-discovery to connect with our Higher Self and inner Light.

1. **Perfection in Being**: We are already perfect and complete as we are, and the journey of self-discovery is the true art of creation.

2. **Nature of Home**: Home can be a place and a feeling, reflecting our inner state and perceptions.

3. **True Observer**: We perceive reality through the filter of our assumptions and interpretations; understanding the true observer within us is crucial.

4. **Self-Acceptance**: Embracing and accepting oneself, with all imperfections, reveals the inherent perfection within us.

5. **Unity and Connection**: We share common aspirations, illusions, and the search for something missing within us, emphasizing our interconnectedness.

6. **Inner Light**: The emptiness within contains the Spark of creation and the Light that dispels darkness, leading to self-discovery and enlightenment.

7. **Freedom and Higher Self**: Becoming one with our Higher Self frees us from illusions, seeking, and mortality, allowing us to remember our true purpose.

The First Encounters With The Unexplainable

Together, these teachings emphasize the importance of recognizing early spiritual experiences, the power of belief in healing, understanding Divine lessons and humor, persevering through challenges, acknowledging interdimensional existence, and embracing the unconditional love of the Divine for a profound and transformative spiritual journey.

1. **Early Spiritual Experiences**: Early encounters with the Divine can set the tone for a lifelong spiritual journey, even if their significance is not immediately understood.

2. **Voice of the Spirit**: Hearing the inner voice of the Spirit, often subtle and peaceful, can provide guidance and comfort in times of need.

3. **Power of Belief and Healing**: The mind's power, bolstered by belief and ritual, can facilitate physical healing in ways that defy conventional medical understanding.

4. **Divine Humor and Lessons**: The Divine can use humor and seemingly inexplicable events to teach profound lessons about the nature of reality and spiritual truths.

5. **Persistence Through Challenges**: Personal hardships and familial struggles can shape one's spiritual path and foster resilience and deeper understanding.

6. **Interdimensional Existence**: Experiencing and recognizing the presence of other dimensions and planes of existence can deepen one's understanding of life and the Divine order.

7. **Unconditional Divine Love**: The Divine presence is characterized by unconditional love, guiding and supporting individuals through all experiences.

Journey to Self-Discovery the Ultimate Truth

Together, these teachings emphasize the importance of recognizing oneness, practicing unconditional love, accepting and forgiving all aspects of life, healing ancestral karma, living authentically, and surrendering to the guidance of the Spirit for profound spiritual growth and fulfillment.

1. **Self-Reflection and Oneness**: Recognize that seeing yourself in others reflects the oneness of all beings; we are all interconnected and share similar struggles and wounds.

2. **Unconditional Love**: Love yourself unconditionally as you love others. What you resist in others mirrors what you cannot accept in yourself.

3. **Acceptance and Forgiveness**: Accepting and forgiving everything in yourself and others leads to healing and

spiritual growth. Judgments create conflict and hinder this process.

4. **Gratitude for Challenges**: Embrace all life experiences, including challenges and injustices, with gratitude as they are crafted for spiritual growth.

5. **Healing Ancestral Karma**: Light Workers are tasked with healing up to seven generations of ancestral karma by embodying and sharing unconditional love and empathy.

6. **Living Authentically**: Free yourself from societal constraints and expectations; embrace your true self, acknowledging that you are already perfect and complete.

7. **Surrender to Spirit**: Stop trying to control life and allow the Spirit to guide you, embracing a passenger-seat perspective in your life's journey.

An Unexpected Visitor One Night

Together, these teachings emphasize the importance of recognizing Divine intervention, maintaining faith and perseverance, experiencing unconditional love, leaving a legacy of service, acknowledging spiritual visitations, practicing gratitude and humility, and receiving support from ancestors for a spiritually enriched life.

1. **Divine Intervention**: Even in the darkest times, the Divine can intervene miraculously to provide guidance and support.

2. **Faith and Perseverance**: Holding onto faith and persevering through hardships can lead to unexpected blessings and spiritual growth.

3. **Unconditional Love**: Experiencing unconditional Divine love can bring profound healing and transformation.

4. **Legacy and Service**: The legacy we leave through acts of kindness and service to others is more valuable than material wealth.

5. **Spiritual Visitations**: Spiritual visitations, such as dreams or visions, can provide comfort, guidance, and affirmation of our life's path.

6. **Gratitude and Humility**: Being grateful and humble, even in difficult circumstances, opens the door for Divine assistance and miracles.

7. **Support from Ancestors**: Ancestors and loved ones who have passed on can still play a significant role in guiding and supporting us from the spiritual realm.

Through The Eyes of a Child

Together, these teachings emphasize the importance of accepting and loving oneself, recognizing the Divine purpose in all experiences, and understanding that true spiritual growth and healing come from within.

1. **Acceptance of Past Experiences**: Accept and release past traumas, understanding that they are invaluable life lessons designed for spiritual growth.

2. **Self-Love and Healing**: Unconditional self-love is essential for reframing past emotional injuries and healing emotional wounds.

3. **Inner Journey**: True emotional and spiritual healing comes from within, not from external sources or intermediaries.

4. **Unity in Spirit**: We are all one in spirit, and the love God has for each of us is unconditional and infinite.

5. **Divine Purpose**: Every experience, no matter how painful, is part of a Divine plan for the soul's development and enlightenment.

6. **Truth and Reality**: The ultimate truth and reality are revealed through spiritual awakening and are beyond earthly comprehension.

7. **Individual Path**: The journey to spiritual enlightenment is personal, and the truth is already within everyone.

Random Events Leading the Way

Together, these teachings emphasize the importance of being open to unexpected Divine encounters, developing an inner connection, exercising faith, recognizing Divine timing, practicing compassion and empathy, being open to receiving guidance from strangers, and embracing the unknown for a spiritually enriched life.

1. **Unexpected Divine Encounters**: Spiritual encounters often happen unexpectedly and in everyday situations, reaffirming the Divine's omnipresence.

2. **Inner Connection**: Developing a deep, still connection with the Higher Self or Spirit can lead to moments of synchronicity and fulfilled intentions.

3. **Faith in Action**: Simple acts of faith, such as asking for help with certainty and gratitude, can yield miraculous results.

4. **Divine Timing**: Divine messages and interventions often occur at precisely the right moment, highlighting the importance of patience and surrender.

5. **Compassion and Empathy**: Encounters with others, especially in moments of vulnerability, can reveal profound spiritual truths and foster empathy and compassion.

6. **Guidance Through Strangers**: The Divine can use strangers as instruments to deliver messages of love and affirmation, reinforcing the interconnectedness of all beings.

7. **Openness to the Unknown**: Being open to the unknown and the seemingly random events in life can lead to profound spiritual insights and growth.

Loosing is Actually Winning

Together, these teachings emphasize the importance of embracing loss, detaching from material and societal expectations, and finding true freedom and inner peace by connecting with our Divine nature.

1. **Embracing Loss**: Losing is a blessing that allows us to understand the deeper meaning of life and reevaluate our beliefs and expectations.

2. **Detachment**: True freedom and peace come from detaching from material and aspirational attachments, enabling us to manifest our true potential.

3. **Reevaluation of Success**: Failure and loss force us to reassess our values and what truly matters, leading to emotional and spiritual development.

4. **Inner Peace and Divine Connection**: Recognizing our Divine nature and trusting in a higher plan brings profound inner peace.

5. **Unconventional Existence**: Breaking free from societal and mental pre-conditioning allows us to find unconventional methods of existence and hidden truths.

6. **True Freedom**: True freedom involves living without fear, free from external impositions, and allowing our soul to guide us instead of our ego.

7. **Living with Intention**: Focusing on experiences rather than material outcomes and letting life flow naturally leads to a fulfilling existence.

Facing Off With the Demonic

Together, these teachings emphasize the importance of recognizing the presence of spiritual warfare, relying on Divine intervention, maintaining strong faith, understanding the power of purification rituals, acknowledging inner Divine power, experiencing spiritual awakening, and embracing universal Divine love for a transformative and empowering spiritual journey.

1. **Presence of Good and Evil**: The reality of spiritual warfare between light and darkness can manifest in physical and supernatural experiences.

2. **Divine Intervention**: The Divine will intervene to protect and guide us in our most desperate moments, reaffirming our faith and spiritual sovereignty.

3. **Power of Faith and Refusal**: The strength to refuse temptations and the power of darkness comes from a deep faith and connection with the Divine.

4. **Role of Purification**: Rituals like foot washing and baptism symbolize purification, humility, and readiness to face spiritual challenges.

5. **Inner Divine Power**: Every individual possesses the Divine spark within, capable of overcoming evil and embodying light.

6. **Spiritual Awakening**: Encounters with the supernatural can catalyze profound spiritual awakening and transformation.

7. **Universal Divine Love**: The Divine's love and protection extend to all, reaffirming our worth and Divine rights as children of the Light.

Our Relationship With Pain

Together, these teachings emphasize the importance of embracing pain as a guide for growth, distinguishing between pain and suffering, and achieving maturity and freedom through acceptance and inner work.

1. **Pain as a Compass**: Pain is a necessary part of the human experience, guiding us to address discrepancies in our lives and bodies.

2. **Acceptance of Pain**: Embracing pain leads to emotional and spiritual maturity by accepting what is

and recognizing the difference between pain and suffering.

3. **Growth Through Pain**: Physical and emotional pain provides opportunities for personal growth and character development.

4. **Overcoming Physical Pain**: Physical pain can be overcome by recognizing that our bodies do not define us and rising above physical ailments.

5. **Emotional Pain and Suffering**: Emotional pain is often self-induced by our perceptions and expectations; acceptance and reframing can prevent suffering.

6. **Inner Work and Awareness**: Emotional and spiritual maturity require inner work and awareness, allowing us to evolve through life's challenges.

7. **Surrender and Freedom**: Surrendering to pain without resistance brings freedom from suffering and helps us master life's lessons.

Deciphering Symbols

Together, these teachings emphasize the importance of recognizing Divine symbolism, maintaining faith, persevering through trials, awakening to spiritual messages, trusting in a higher plan, and being of service to others for a transformative spiritual journey.

1. **Divine Symbolism**: Recognizing and understanding symbols in our lives can provide guidance and affirm our spiritual journey.

2. **Ancestral Connections**: Our ancestors' influence and love play a significant role in guiding and supporting us through life's challenges.

3. **Faith and Devotion**: Maintaining faith and devotion, even in dark times, leads to Divine intervention and spiritual growth.

4. **Perseverance Through Trials**: Enduring hardships and trials with perseverance strengthens our connection with the Divine and fosters personal transformation.

5. **Unwavering Faith**: Trusting in a higher plan, despite seeming setbacks, eventually fulfills our purpose and Divine will.

6. **Spiritual Awakening**: Spiritual awakening often involves recognizing the signs and messages around us and responding with humility and acceptance.

7. **Role of Service**: Being of service to others and fulfilling our commitments brings profound spiritual rewards and growth.

Our Relationship With Reality

Together, these teachings emphasize the necessity of self-awareness, inner change, and maintaining integrity to create a balanced and fulfilling life, individually and within society.

1. **Inner Change for Outer Change**: Lasting change in the world begins with a significant change in how we relate to ourselves.

2. **Reflection and Self-Awareness**: Reality acts as a mirror, pointing out what is not working in our relationship with ourselves.

3. **Importance of Self-Relationships**: The most important relationships are with our Creator and ourselves, which impact how we show up in the world.

4. **Self-Discovery Through Adversity**: Confronting undesired outcomes and failures leads to self-discovery and necessary change.

5. **Holistic Development**: True success involves balancing physical, psychological, emotional, and spiritual aspects of life.

6. **Divine Connection**: Healing and self-worth come from understanding our Divine sovereignty and our place in the cosmic tapestry.

7. **Societal Reflection**: How we treat ourselves correlates with how we allow society to treat us and others.

8. **Living Righteously**: Honoring ourselves and others through a righteous life and maintaining integrity is essential for a prosperous society.

Reciprocity of Shadows

Together, these teachings emphasize the importance of unexpected guidance, surrendering to the Divine, practicing gratitude and acceptance, emotional healing, listening to spiritual messages, understanding purpose, and trusting in Divine timing for a fulfilling and transformative spiritual journey.

1. **Unexpected Guidance**: The Divine often sends unexpected messengers and events to guide us on our spiritual journey, especially when we are not actively seeking them.

2. **Surrender to the Divine**: Letting go of personal aspirations and surrendering to the Divine's guidance can lead to profound spiritual growth and understanding.

3. **Gratitude and Acceptance**: Being grateful for all experiences, even the challenging ones, is essential for spiritual development and creating a positive, abundant life.

4. **Emotional Healing and Self-Worth**: Encounters with others can facilitate emotional healing and help restore our self-worth, especially after traumatic experiences.

5. **Listening to Spiritual Messages**: Paying attention to spiritual messages and signs can provide clarity and direction in our lives.

6. **Purpose and Meaning**: Understanding that our life's journey has a greater purpose and that every experience is an opportunity for growth and learning.

7. **Divine Timing and Trust**: Trusting in Divine timing and allowing life to unfold naturally can lead to profound realizations and spiritual awakenings.

I am What I am

Together, these teachings emphasize the profound impact of thoughts and words on our reality, the importance of inner awareness, and the journey toward self-identification and spiritual enlightenment.

1. **Thoughts Shape Existence**: Our thoughts dictate our reality; we become what we think.

2. **Conscious Awareness**: Elevating consciousness above autopilot thoughts reveals the true nature of reality.

3. **Power of Words**: Words construct reality, with "I am" being the most potent self-identification.

4. **Inner Journey and Grace**: True wisdom and spiritual mastery come from within and are often a result of Grace.

5. **Subjective Reality**: Perceptions of truth and reality are subjective and vary between individuals.

6. **Self-Identification**: How we identify ourselves with words influences our experiences and actions.

7. **Embracing Lack and Pain**: True growth and character development often come through experiencing and overcoming lack and pain.

8. **Divine Connection**: Finding the Divine within oneself is essential for spiritual growth and enlightenment.

Divine Encounters

Together, these teachings emphasize the importance of supernatural guidance, surrender, embracing the Divine, fasting and purification, personal revelation, unity with the Divine, and living authentically for profound spiritual growth and transformation.

1. **Supernatural Guidance**: Heightened states of consciousness and mystical experiences often occur during early morning meditations, providing telepathic downloads and inspiration.

2. **Surrender and Letting Go**: To progress spiritually, one must relinquish all emotional attachments and

surrender entirely to the Divine, allowing for personal transformation and higher awareness.

3. **Embracing the Divine**: Experiencing Divine encounters involves accepting guidance and allowing the Holy Spirit to dictate a greater purpose beyond personal desires and expectations.

4. **Fasting and Purification**: Fasting and consuming natural, unprocessed foods enhance spiritual awareness and open channels to higher frequencies and realms.

5. **Personal Revelation**: Everyone's spiritual journey is unique, and Divine encounters provide personal guidance and insights tailored to one's specific path.

6. **Unity with the Divine**: Realizing our oneness brings peace, understanding, and the ability to navigate life's challenges with Divine support and wisdom.

7. **Living Authentically**: Embracing a lifestyle that aligns with spiritual teachings and natural order facilitates deeper communion with the Divine and greater personal fulfillment.

Our Relationship With Nature

Together, these teachings emphasize the importance of reconnecting with nature, embracing sustainable living, adhering to a natural diet, questioning societal norms, and applying first principles of thinking to foster a healthier relationship with the environment and our own well-being.

1. **Cultural Conditioning**: From childhood, we are conditioned by society and family to adopt certain

views and practices regarding our relationship with the environment, often detaching from a natural way of living.

2. **Symbiotic Relationship with Nature**: True harmony with Nature involves recognizing and embracing the symbiotic relationship we have with the environment, which provides us with sustenance in a natural, unaltered form.

3. **Sustainable Living**: Living sustainably requires questioning the status quo and seeking ways to minimize harm to the environment, understanding the closed-loop system of our planet.

4. **Natural Diet**: Our natural diet consists of raw, unprocessed foods that can be gathered directly from Nature, such as fruits, vegetables, nuts, and seeds, without human intervention or industrial processing.

5. **Impact of Industrialization**: The industrialization of food production and consumption has led to environmental degradation and health issues, detaching us from our natural diet and causing long-term harm to both our bodies and the ecosystem.

6. **Questioning Norms**: Challenging societal norms and questioning the validity of modern practices can lead to a greater understanding of our true relationship with Nature and foster healthier living.

7. **First Principles Thinking**: Applying first principles thinking to our dietary and lifestyle choices helps uncover fundamental truths about what is natural and beneficial for our health and the environment.

Maximizing Life's Pleasures

Together, these teachings emphasize the importance of understanding life's purpose, embracing all experiences, surrendering to the Divine, living in the now, achieving integrity, focusing on inner being, and practicing unconditional love for a fulfilling and spiritually enriched life.

1. **Purpose of Life**: Life's experiences are designed to teach us the lessons we signed up for, guiding us toward greater self-realization and understanding of who we truly are.

2. **Embrace Experiences**: Accepting and embracing all experiences, including pain and suffering, allows us to learn and grow, advancing to higher levels of spiritual awareness.

3. **Power of Surrender**: True co-creation and fulfillment come from surrendering and letting go, trusting that the Divine knows our desires and has our best interests at heart.

4. **Living in the Now**: Living in the present moment and appreciating life as it is helps us align with our higher purpose and recognize the Divine timing in our journey.

5. **Integrity and Authenticity**: Achieving integrity at all levels—keeping our word, aligning actions with feelings, and behaving consistently with our true self—is essential for spiritual growth.

6. **Inner Being Over Material Pursuits**: Focusing on inner development rather than material achievements leads to lasting fulfillment and alignment with our true purpose.

7. **Unconditional Love**: Mastering the art of unconditional love and letting go of ego-driven desires unlocks the true power within us and reveals the essence of the Divine.

Sacred Medicines

Together, these teachings emphasize the importance of inner guidance, alternative healing methods, non-attachment to societal norms, and the continuous inner work required for profound personal transformation and service to others.

1. **Healing Through Pain**: Facing deep emotional and childhood wounds head-on is essential for healing and growth.

2. **Inner Guidance**: Listening to inner guidance and spiritual whispers can lead to transformative healing experiences.

3. **Alternative Healing**: Sacred medicines like psilocybin and Ayahuasca offer profound healing and insights, often more effective than traditional therapies.

4. **Non-Attachment to Societal Norms**: Breaking free from societal labels and expectations is necessary for genuine self-discovery and healing.

5. **Self-Determination and Inner Work**: True healing requires self-determination, inner work, and the integration of wisdom gained from sacred ceremonies.

6. **Empathy and Service**: Healing oneself allows for greater empathy and the ability to assist others on their healing journeys.

7. **Recognizing the Wounded Healer Syndrome**: It's crucial to use sacred medicines as tools for growth

rather than becoming dependent on them as a coping mechanism.

The Act of Renunciation

Together, these teachings emphasize the importance of renunciation, unconditional love, spiritual connections, Divine healing, understanding symbolism, unity with the Divine, and living authentically for a transformative and fulfilling life.

1. **Renunciation and Transformation**: Letting go of old emotional attachments and identities allows for the birth of a new, authentic self.

2. **Unconditional Love**: Showing unconditional love and gratitude to those in our lives helps us embrace and learn from all experiences.

3. **Spiritual Connections**: Meeting individuals on similar spiritual journeys can provide profound exchanges of wisdom and healing.

4. **Divine Healing**: Spiritual experiences and visions can lead to deep emotional healing and resetting of past hurts.

5. **Symbolism and Guidance**: Recognizing and understanding spiritual symbols, such as the lotus flower, can provide guidance and affirm spiritual victories.

6. **Unity with the Divine**: Realizing the oneness with the Divine brings peace and understanding of our True nature.

7. **Living Authentically**: Embracing our true selves and honoring our bodies as temples lead to a more authentic and fearless existence.

Navigating Towards Choiceless Observation

Together, these teachings emphasize the importance of inner stillness, Divine guidance, non-attachment, continuous learning, and embracing community and the unknown for spiritual growth and fulfillment.

1. **Inner Equilibrium and Stillness**: Achieving inner peace and equilibrium requires embracing stillness and detaching from the ego.

2. **Divine Guidance**: Being open to Divine guidance can lead to unexpected, meaningful connections and opportunities for personal growth.

3. **Non-Attachment**: Detaching from material possessions and sharing openly with others fosters a more profound sense of connection and fulfillment.

4. **Continuous Learning**: Spiritual growth constantly involves trials and lessons that test our understanding and commitment.

5. **Choiceless Observation**: Embracing a state of choiceless observation allows us to navigate life's challenges with clarity and acceptance.

6. **Community and Sharing**: True fulfillment come from living in harmony with others, sharing resources, and creating supportive communities.

7. **Embracing the Unknown**: Remaining open to the unknown and embracing life's surprises can lead to profound spiritual experiences and insights.

Embracing the Divine

Together, these teachings emphasize the importance of Divine connection, inner healing, embracing change, self-love, meaningful connections, recognizing spiritual signs, and understanding our purpose and unity with all creation.

1. **Divine Connection**: Experiencing the Divine in everyday life involves being open to spiritual guidance and recognizing moments of profound connection.

2. **Inner Healing**: True healing involves emptying oneself of ego and allowing the Spirit to work through us to heal others emotionally and spiritually.

3. **Embracing Change**: Transformation and growth often require embracing change, facing discomfort, and stepping into the unknown.

4. **Self-Love and Unconditional Love**: Healing others often begins with self-love and extends to sharing unconditional love with those around us.

5. **Shared Experiences**: Meaningful connections and shared experiences can lead to profound spiritual insights and personal growth.

6. **Symbolism and Signs**: Recognizing spiritual symbols and signs, such as the dragonfly, can guide our spiritual journey and affirm our connection to the Divine.

7. **Purpose and Unity**: Understanding our purpose and experiencing unity with all of creation helps us recognize our Divine essence and interconnectedness.

Embracing Our Inborn Identity

Together, these teachings emphasize the importance of embracing our true identity, pursuing our passions, surrendering to Divine timing, discovering our inner gifts, balancing free will and predestination, breaking free from societal impositions, and trusting greater forces for a fulfilling and authentic life.

1. **Destiny by Birthright**: Our true identity and destiny are defined by our inborn qualities and Divine design, not societal expectations or ego-driven pursuits.

2. **The Role of Passion**: Pursuing one's true passion leads to fulfillment and co-creation, while forcing oneself into societal molds results in dissatisfaction and suffering.

3. **Divine Timing and Surrender**: Letting go of control and surrendering to Divine timing allows for serendipitous and karmic experiences that guide us to our true path.

4. **Inner Gifts and Integrity**: Focusing on discovering and embracing our inner gifts aligns us with our true purpose, leading to meaningful contributions and inner peace.

5. **Free Will and Predestination**: While we have free will, specific predestined experiences shape our lives, providing necessary lessons for spiritual growth.

6. **Breaking Free from Societal Impositions**: Rejecting imposed career paths and societal norms allows us to follow our true calling and live authentically.

7. **Trust in Greater Forces**: Trusting that greater forces guide our lives helps us embrace uncertainty and align with our Divine purpose.

Transforming Into The Void

Together, these teachings emphasize the importance of embracing transformation, entering a state of flow, co-creating with the Divine, surrendering the ego, living authentically, and recognizing the power of Divine manifestation for a spiritually enriched and fulfilling life.

1. **Embrace a Blank Slate**: The potential of a blank piece of paper symbolizes the human spirit's ability to transform and create anew, shedding old identities and embracing new ones.

2. **Shattering Self-Concepts**: Breaking free from limiting self-concepts allows for personal growth and self-discovery, leading to a deeper understanding of our true purpose.

3. **State of Flow**: Emptiness and simplicity enable us to enter a state of flow, where we can tap into higher consciousness and achieve significant creative and intellectual breakthroughs.

4. **Co-Creation with the Divine**: Engaging in communion with the Divine helps us realize a higher purpose and transform into our true selves, guided by a Divine blueprint.

5. **Surrendering Ego**: Letting go of ego-driven desires and accepting ourselves as we are, allows for a deeper

connection with the Divine and a more fulfilling existence.

6. **Living Authentically**: Engaging in life's affairs with unconditional love and detachment from outcomes fosters a state of co-creation and mastery, leading to unexpected and profound results.

7. **Divine Manifestation**: Recognizing the Divine spark within us and surrendering to the Divine's guidance helps us achieve outcomes far beyond our ego's comprehension.

Reflections of Self

Together, these teachings emphasize the importance of recognizing our judgments as reflections, engaging in introspection, and fostering unconditional love and acceptance to achieve spiritual growth and unity.

1. **Judgment as Reflection**: Our judgments of others reflect aspects of ourselves that need healing; unconditional love and acceptance are the keys to escaping this cycle.

2. **Introspection and Inner Work**: True wisdom and self-improvement come from introspection, forgiveness, and aligning with the Truth within ourselves.

3. **Duality and Oneness**: Understanding that we are all One in Spirit helps us heal ourselves and others by recognizing the shared Divine essence.

4. **Self-Realization and Spiritual Practices**: Awakening to our true identity eliminates the need for external spiritual practices, as the Truth resides within us.

5. **Nonjudgmental Awareness:** Achieving a nonjudgmental state signifies resolving inner conflicts, which allows us to help others on their spiritual journeys.

6. **Service to Others**: Serving others unconditionally and sharing spiritual wisdom enhances our own spiritual growth and connection with the Divine.

7. **Inner Peace and Higher Awareness**: Attaining inner peace and higher awareness involves questioning societal norms and seeking the Light within.

About The Journey Begins Within

Exploring the Depths of the Self and the Universe

In "The Journey Begins Within," readers embark on an enlightening voyage through the mind, spirit, and cosmos landscapes. Authored by SAVI, a seeker of truth and wisdom, the book unfolds as a deeply personal narrative, interwoven with profound insights gleaned from a life rich in experiences and metaphysical exploration. SAVI invites us on a quest for external discovery, inward reflection, and growth, challenging us to confront and embrace the depths of our being.

Drawing upon his journey of spiritual awakening and the lessons learned from encounters that defy ordinary explanation, SAVI crafts a compelling case for the pursuit of gnosis - the direct knowledge of the divine without intermediation. He presents a tapestry of stories and reflections, ranging from the whispers of the spirit that guide him to the tangible impact of the metaphysical on the physical realm. Through "Gleaned Insights from Gnostic Exploration," SAVI shares wisdom accumulated from extraordinary events, dietary disciplines, and practices such as fasting, offering readers a roadmap to navigate their spiritual landscapes.

This book is more than just a collection of experiences; it's an invitation to embark on a journey to our Heavenly Father and His Holy Spirit. It's about finding the divine within and recognizing that our true identity and purpose are intricately linked to a higher, spiritual realm. SAVI dedicates his work to his earthly father, whose influence and guidance have been a beacon in his life and his girlfriend, embodying the message that our paths to the divine can vary as much as our preferences in consuming wisdom.

"The Journey Begins Within" is not just a book; it's a gateway to a deeper understanding of the self and the universe. It beckons readers to explore the unknown with courage, openness, and a heart ready to receive the boundless love and wisdom within us all.

"The end....

... is your beginning!"

-SAVI

About SAVI

An Unconventional Truth Seeker

SAVI is a spiritual explorer and author of "The Journey Begins Within," where he chronicles his profound adventures through the realms of consciousness and the metaphysical. A dreamer by choice, SAVI has lived an extraordinary life marked by an unwavering quest for the ultimate truth. His path, defined by integrity, high ideals, and a stubborn refusal to conform to societal expectations, has led him through enlightening discoveries and humbling dead ends.

His experiences, ranging from personal trials to encounters with the Divine, are shared to guide others toward their spiritual awakening. SAVI's life story is a testament to the belief that we are more than the sum of our experiences; the memories we leave on the paths of others genuinely define us. His work invites readers to embark on their journey of self-discovery, encouraging them to seek a deeper connection with the universe and the spirit within.

Made in the USA
Columbia, SC
19 August 2024

Our Relationship With Nature

When did we forget we belong in it?

When we are born into a culture, family, and society, we are, from childhood, shown what we take for granted: our relationship with the environment surrounding us and, within that, the quality and sources of the food we eat. We do not question much. We have shown our parents some disdain for certain foods, which they eventually force us to eat, but we primarily become carbon copies of our parents or tutors. Whether they were blissfully blind due to their upbringing or not, very few in the world are lucky to have been born into a consciously awakened family that lives in harmony with the natural surroundings, as primarily humankind has detached from a healthy relationship with Nature long ago since the beginning of the industrial revolution. And before you go ahead and label me as an environmentalist, a vegan, or any depiction of what you deem this article to be, you would do yourself a great favor and humanity to keep your identifications at bay. I have transcended a significant number of mental constructs for you to limit me in your mind, as you will miss the key points that I would like to bring to the forefront of your awareness. Our relationship with Nature is significantly more encompassing than just our diet and how we live on this planet. Once we take our rightful place within Nature, some, if not all, of our Spiritual gifts may come into play within our awareness. There could be more reasons than economic or straightforward ignorance about current affairs.

During my life, I have visited many homes of others from different socioeconomic backgrounds worldwide, from poor people living in wooden shacks with dirt floors to billionaire mansions with extremely lavish interiors and everything in between. Although some were tidier than others, there was one common element: the bathroom was separate from the kitchen. In other words, nobody eats where one defecates, and for good reason. What we put out tends to be incompatible with what we put into our bodies, and as far as I am aware, this fact applies to all cultures in the world that I have seen or experienced. I always say that the most profound truths are hidden in plain sight. We, as humans, also repeat this pattern in our interaction with and within "Mother Nature." Somehow, what we put into it is incompatible with what it gives us. Yet we believe it is our inherent right to continue to do our business whichever way we want or are told we must. Nature provides for us in a never-ending loop of abundance, yet not without repercussions for our actions. Well, it is only a matter of time and scale before a closed-loop system shifts its dynamic equilibrium based on the inputs it gets.

The issue is that if the system is extensive and the individual inputs are minimal in comparison, direct measurements can't accurately pinpoint cause-and-effect relations, making it hard to correlate the identification of culprits with the issues. These points are not about the arguments of global warming, as it has already been proven that our atmosphere has had several glacial and greenhouse cycles without human intervention. But this is about *humanity's blindness to the fact that we live in a closed-loop spaceship system*, floating in a vacuum, traveling at 67,000 MPH within a galaxy, traveling at 2,237,000 MPH relative to other galaxies. Our spaceship has a nuclear fusion reactor that provides all the energy needs of our space travel, along with our gravitational anti-collision force field, called the planetary solar system, and a life-sustainable biosphere within the so-called atmosphere. Indeed, it is a masterpiece of bioengineering and physics if you ask me. I love to chat face-to-face with the aeronautical engineer capable of creating such complex systems and interactions. Anyway, I digress but read between the lines of my sarcasm.

As a species, we live, reproduce, and go generations without raising awareness of these basic facts. We solely focus on our survival without questioning how we fit into this closed-loop. As we explore our relationship with the *"mothership"* more granularly, we forget or do not realize that certain symbiotic relationships exist to provide for our natural sustenance. Still, our egos and identifications cloudy our eyes to what is true and what is not. We create industries that go against the planet's well-being and, eventually, ourselves. We pollute the surroundings and our bodies with the outputs we produce and do not see the interrelationships of the closed-loop system until the damage is done. Then, we figure out more industries to counter our initial actions, from unnecessary medicine in the case of several chronic diseases that can be avoided through proper nutrition to environmental systems that try to undo the pollution of others.

When you open your eyes to a greater Truth, you question the status quo and distinguish what is real from fiction. As a species, we have detached from what is factual in an effort to self-preserve our advancement within the societal hierarchy, with no regard for the greater good, simply because we are not taught the bigger picture from childhood. So, I started to question myself and everything around me to establish what would be a plausible, healthy relationship within the inner and outer ecosystems. I realized that, first and foremost, regardless of how much I tried to separate myself from my outputs when the scale was large enough, these would impact my inputs. Therefore, whatever I am here to do, I must do it responsibly to avoid being selfish and maintain integrity in everything I do or choose to embody. Henceforth, I must experience unconditional love for myself and reflect it unto others through my choices and the effect on the closed-loop system. In this case, it meant I must change my core belief system, including the software package I downloaded throughout my childhood. It was clear to me that an upgrade in perception was needed. Unlike Elon Musk, the driving force behind Space X and Tesla, who also believed in first principles thinking and that humanity is too far gone to change. In Elon's view, we are in a spiral of self-destruction; contrary to him, I have been blessed not to attain his success, allowing me to ferment and ponder more profound existential questions longer in a quest for self-realization. Only through the chaos of trial and error can one delve deeper into the first principles method in confronting failures and determine what is true versus subjectivity. If what is true is to be adopted as a general law for humanity, it must apply to every aspect of the greater whole and not only to the individual parts. I want to share some of the questions I have pondered for over a decade since my awakening began, and I was called to reflect upon my existence on a natural plane.

Why are we the only species in the spaceship that does not eat its natural diet or live in a symbiotic relationship within its designated environment? What is a natural way to provide food for our bodies? What is food, and what is a product of our imagination and beliefs? I figured there had to be something I was unaware of beyond my carnivore, omnivore food preferences from my Argentine—Italian descent. Why would there be foods I would lose my domain on when to stop consuming versus others I would naturally feel satiated from and not overeat? What wasn't I being taught in my family and school? Why were most elders dying of chronic diseases or cancers? There had to be a common nexus between the unseen and the experienced circumstances. So, I decided in my early thirties when I was prescribed my first pressure medication, and the cardiologist's response was, "*You will take this for the rest of your life*," to view it as an unacceptable outcome for me.

Doctors are also the result of their environment, and although they do a fantastic job for society, for the most part, they treat symptoms, not the cause. Very few I have come across open their eyes beyond the initial medical training and are intellectually curious enough to seek alternative answers. Yet regulatory bodies and compliance boards quickly shut down any spur of individual thinking. Discoveries take decades to percolate through the stiffness of the self-imposed system, and in the wake, millions die unnecessarily complicated deaths as the one certainty is that we will eventually all die; the question remains: can we do it less painfully and naturally? The truth is yes, but it may not suit established businesses.

So now that we have determined a direct correlation between what we put in and what we get out of a closed-ended system, what is the most suitable means by which we can interact with said system? At the very essence, our own body is also a subsystem within the greater ecosystem, and whether you believe in Divine creation or evolution, both philosophies and everything in between dictate that a human organism must directly interact with the system it belongs to. Hence, we must have a natural mechanism to fulfill our existence straight from the "*factory*," our mother's womb, without any exogenous requirement for tools or methods. When we are born, we are meant to lactate from the milk our mothers provide. There is a reason why biological females have breasts; it is a sorry situation for a society in which this is even a debate point, but believe it or not, it has everything to do with our detachment from reality and our relationship with Nature.

We know that most babies should be capable of drinking breast milk from day one. It should be easy enough. Let's move on. Now, what happens after any mammalian species stops lactating? They eat their everyday sustenance provided by Nature without adulteration, a fact for all, regardless of the source. So, whatever the natural human source of food is, it stands to reason that both children and adults should be able to eat it without any necessary modification from the source. Right? Unless you believe you are some alien species who were genetically modified and implanted into the ecosystem, the prior statement applies.

We are continuing to dive into other first principles. What are plausible natural food sources for humankind: fruits, vegetables, mushrooms, nuts, seeds, animal flesh, milk, honey, and eggs? Perhaps there are a few subspecies or classifications, more like plankton or algae, but we'll get into the main points in a minute. If you are still with me and I haven't lost you, you must realize that any deviation from the prior facts is not our natural food source. Examples are anything that requires some process or modification by the human hand to be ingested, which *implies these are not our natural sustenance*. Although we survive and can eat it sporadically, it stands to reason that we are not meant to eat it long term, or our system will break down for many reasons. So, in essence, one can avoid a selfish attitude and determine that if we are to live in harmony within the large ecosystem of the *"Spaceship Earth,"* then we need to eat what is intended for us to live within the system and not what our ego dictates, distorted tastebuds or will desires. This fact should immediately eliminate everything that was somehow created by the intervention of human intellect, meaning any alteration of the natural state of food *is an unnatural choice that has a negative implication for both the internal body systems and the greater ecosystem.* So, in basic terms, processing either by heat, cold, mechanical, or chemical alterations distorts the natural state of food for us to eat and, at its core, its essence. These are unnatural foods for our species and force upon our own body a potential issue as its core design did not intend for said substances to be ingested in that manner, bringing undesired consequences and, in general, the causation of many avoidable medical conditions.

Let's keep going down the rabbit hole we are exploring to establish that there must be a natural order in our existence through evolution or Divine design. We established that either way, there must be a natural symbiotic relationship between all the moving parts of a closed-loop system and the consequences of the inputs and outputs. We also establish that the ecosystem must already provide humanity's natural diet unadulterated. Finally, all mammals adapt from birth to be fed by Nature from a nursing mother. Yes, there are exceptions to babies born within countless circumstances or issues, but again, we are establishing the first principle to seek the Truth. There will be naysayers till the end of time, so one must welcome their opposition, gently love them unconditionally, and let them exist in their ways. Ultimately, it is their birthright to seek expression; we are not here to change anyone. We are here to uncover the Truth and let the Light of the Truth shine upon each one to make the change required.

So, after this quick recap, let's focus on the next logical iteration of the concepts. If we are equipped from birth to sustain ourselves like all other animal species in the spaceship, then we must be able to nourish ourselves from what our bodies can achieve after lactating. We have two hands and two legs as the primary means to gather and bring food into our mouths in a natural state. And I trust you agree with these facts regardless of your preferences and lifestyles.

In other words, if we are hunters, we should be able to eat our natural prey, and when we identify it, our mouths should salivate like the big carnivores or every carnivore subspecies. I don't know about you, but having been an avid grill master and meat consumer from Argentina, I have eaten a steak daily for several decades; never once did I feel inclined to take a bite of the raw meat before adding copious amounts of salt and grilling it. I am also an avid fisherman and diver, with countless killings to my name either by hand, knife, spears, or firearms of both land and water animals of all sorts. I never felt compelled to eat the fresh kill without prior processing or cooking, including sushi. So, there is some basic incongruency between the fact that my body naturally repudiates the eating of freshly killed animal proteins of all sorts and what I was taught to believe since birth by my family and society.

Furthermore, like all carnivore animals, I should be able to kill my prey with my extremities and mouth. The only animals I've caught with my hands in my lifetime are mollusks, lobsters, lizards, insects, and chickens. Although I managed to get my hands on all the other larger animals like pigs, cows, etc., I could not kill with my bare hands. But even the few I mentioned did not appeal to me in a raw form, so basically, unless cooked or prepared extensively, they are not meant to be a recurring food within the closed ecosystem we all belong to. Some of you may rightfully argue that we discovered fire approximately 400,000 years ago and evolved to utilize it. Still, my question to these people is, have you tried to light a fire with some stones, which must be a particular kind not readily available, or just friction from two pieces of very dry wood?

I am confident that after you try it, you won't argue that it is significantly more accessible and desirous to our species to eat an apple if readily available than to chase something running away from us, kill it, process it, light a fire with hopefully dry kindling or rocks, cook it, and eat it. *Unnatural means of survival came about as an adaptation to unnatural environments and ways of life, such as colder climates that do not provide our natural sustenance.* If you still have a logical argument against these facts, watch a Discovery Channel video of a carnivore animal hunting down its prey. I invite you to replicate it in real life. Go to a farm, chase something you usually eat in the grocery store, kill it with your hands, and bite on it right there and then with no further processing. Please videotape yourself and upload it to the internet; you will make history as the first confirmed human-carnivore.

Now, we have established that we are not meant to eat animal flesh in the natural order of things within the spaceship's closed-loop. This undermines many entrenched industries and lobbies simply trying to sustain their interests despite the well-being of humanity and the overall ecosystem. We are not even close to being done here since this is but a scratch on the surface of the blinders humanity has placed upon itself from the inception of our modern society. By now, we are done with all cooked, packaged products. Let's focus on the things we can collect with our limbs, primarily things that do not run away from us and are abundant and easy to find. Fruits, when in season, green plants and compatible foliage with our digestive system as we are not herbivores either, meaning we do not eat grass like cows, horses, etc.

What are grains, then, but the seeds of different types of grasses? Is there any need for these in our day-to-day diets if we can't even get the nutrients contained in them without extensive mechanical processing or cooking? The short answer is no. We are not meant to eat like cows and horses either, and hence, unless you go to a corn or wheat field and can chew directly on a corncob or wheat kernels as they come straight out of the plants, we are not meant to eat them. That removes another substantial percentage of the grocery aisles in modern societies and frees a significant amount of our agricultural land.

We keep destroying the ecosystem by occupying the closed-looped spaceship for produce and sources of sustenance that are not even the ones we are meant to eat. How crazy has the whole world become? Has nobody stopped and questioned any of these basic facts to determine the truth? Clearly not!

So, what is left as a natural food source in the grocery store is negligible compared to the perceived norm. Humans are meant to eat raw, unprocessed natural produce provided by Mother Nature when in season, locally grown, and harvested when ripe. Unfortunately, as a society, we have overlooked these basic premises. In the US, we eat fruit or produce removed from trees or taken from the soil weeks in advance in the name of logistics and economies of scale, and we are thus deprived of the nutrients Nature intended for us. Nuts and seeds are salted, roasted, or industrially processed somehow, and efforts are made to generate products that trigger addictive behaviors, ultimately driving demand and overconsumption while neglecting the health of the human body and the ecosystem it is meant to live within. Essentially, we have become so detached from our natural state of being that we continue to harm our body's internal systems and the natural ecosystem within the closed-loop system we call Mother Earth. I am not here to advocate one diet over another, one medical system over another, or to dictate what we should eat. *I aim to raise awareness, enabling you to draw conclusions and broaden your perspectives.* The more we allow each person to discover the truth for themselves, the easier the shift to a sustainable, symbiotic way of life will be. Imposing our beliefs on others will only create resistance, leaving us stagnant. While new ideas will face endless opposition, remember that we do not live in the isolated bubble they made us believe since birth. The truth is right before our eyes. We are an inherent part of this ecosystem, naturally equipped to nourish our bodies and live what should have been an everyday life. You then face a choice, similar to Neo's in the Matrix movie: *continue being oblivious, accepting the lies you've been fed, or choose to awaken to your true potential, ready to face the consequences that come with it.*

The truth will be so, regardless of your beliefs. Apply the first-principle logic to your questions, and you will find the answers. What about the rest? The list needs to be more extensive than this text is meant to encompass, but you will begin to understand once you ask yourself these questions.

Do mammals lactate past a certain age? Are there other cross-lactation examples in Nature besides the human dairy industry? What about eggs? How many eggs would we encounter by walking in nature during a week's stroll if we walked freely on Earth? Would these eggs be unfertilized, like those in grocery stores, or would they contain a developing embryo when found? Do you find cracking an egg and eating an unhatched baby bird appealing, as reptilians do, or are you generally disgusted by the thought alone?

I found the Truth long ago and adapted my life to follow evolution or the Divine natural order. Why aren't you doing the same already, and what are the implications for your long-term health and society? The short answer is that you are too busy fighting for the day-to-day needs, and in the survival struggle within the socioeconomic order, there is little time or room for independent thinking. Whether this is by intended design by a sinister, dark, unknown force or simply by serendipitous design is unknown to me. *It takes a great mind and a strong will to go against the grain and the fabric of the perceived reality even to ask intelligent questions, let alone find the answers.*

Don't expect extraordinary if you are ordinary!

Maximizing Life's Pleasures

The Art of Unconscious Appreciation

What if I were to reveal the secret of all secrets about the purpose of life? But most importantly, what if I told you that the whole of creation is yielding at every second of your existence to provide you with the experiences you signed up to receive since the beginning of time? What if there was a secret code or pact you made with your Heavenly Father for this and every prior one of your lifetimes, through which you would ascend into a greater realization of who you indeed are? What if everything around you in this lifetime was ideally provided for you - not how you wanted it to happen, but how you needed it instead?

What if instead of complaining about the experiences, you embraced them wholeheartedly, fulfilling your life's journey and finding your purpose? What if pain and suffering were only road signs from your soul, directing you to focus on what you are not seeing or focusing on? Once you surrender to the journey instead of constantly fighting it, you graduate to a higher level, ready for the next challenge. Each level brings a divine act of grace as a welcome gift and a way for the Spirit to tell you, *"Good job, my Son or Daughter of the Light."* Within the duality of this world or realm, darkness must exist to provide the contrast required for gaining insights and awareness of our growth. Each lesson, customized to perfection by reality in ways we often fail to identify, generally contains several aspects that push us from the physical planes of existence to the psychological and, later, spiritual ones. As we overcome each level, like in a virtual computer game, we attain *"superpowers"* to easily see the lessons that we later apply and share with other fellow gamers. This sharing helps them achieve the video game level much quicker because playing with your best friends is always more fun than being alone. You want them by your side on the next level.

Returning to actualizing our desires, there is a secret not revealed to many. Most of you may have heard about the power of visualization, living in the now, and even feeling and acting as if your wishes have already been fulfilled. However, what many new age gurus out there often forget to mention, simply because they may not have experienced it themselves, is that the true superpower that unlocks your co-creation abilities is surrendering and letting go. Why do you think your Heavenly Father not only knows your every desire before you even ask for it but also has your best interests at heart? When we forget these critically elevated states of awareness and descend into a mundane 3D existence within the dreamed state called life, we lose the perspective of the Enlightened ones. You understand what I mean if you have already managed to break free from your slumber. If you have not yet experienced higher states of consciousness, do not worry; you inevitably will, either in this lifetime or during your subsequent ones, as it is within your Divine destiny to ascend through each stage until you merge back with the Source. When we fall back into living an everyday 3D life, the most crucial aspect to remember is that everything is happening for us, not to us. This understanding contains the key to allowing the lesson to show us what our Spirit or Soul has signed up to achieve or learn in this lifetime. The quicker we embrace the pain of the situation, the faster we can see the lesson's objectives across all three planes of existence: the physical, the psychological, and the spiritual. We are in a never-ending hide-and-seek game between us and the higher realms. Unfortunately, many, if not the majority, are too absorbed in the survival race to gain enough awareness to see these patterns within life.

Once, when someone outside of the script of our movie stands there with their *"Spiritual eye open"* and sees the lesson we are going through, they can point to us as the *"hidden Master"* in plain sight and release us from the level we may be stuck in. Again, this brother or sister capable of giving us this shortcut can only do so because they have already mastered that specific lesson or level. For them, it is almost like child's play to unlock it within us by pointing out what is evident to them. The easiest of analogies is that our Souls are like tuning forks. When another similar one is close by vibrating at a higher frequency, we start resonating ourselves with theirs. In what could almost be described as a magical fashion, we retune ourselves to overcome the lesson we are confronting.

Every soul in our lives is there for an exchange of sorts; we are all students and masters of each other. We are all running a much bigger movie script dictated by the Powers of Being throughout eternity, and the casting call was at the beginning of time itself.

So, within these essential secrets lie the opportunity to truly live a fulfilling life not from the achievements of the material but the wins from within us. We all start at the same starting line at birth; many solely get stuck on the material and physical aspects of their development, but only some answer the calls from within and rise to higher levels within the game of life. As with any video game, each level has its own hidden traps, difficulties, and, most importantly, challenges, bringing invaluable lessons that most likely all will provide us with countless opportunities to not only pay any karmic debts from the past but also develop ourselves into Beings of Light which is our true essence at the deepest of our cores. Within these last levels, all there is to experience is the absolute stillness of total detachment from the ego, and within the surrender of the acceptance of what is and the letting go of what is not, the most powerful of forces ever created is unleashed, whose driving force is compassion and whose name is Unconditional Love.

Once one masters this level, we understand the authentic fabric of the Universe itself. This reveals to us the Sacred Union of the Trinity and that there is nothing outside our Heavenly Father, who dwells at the core of our being and is awaiting each of us to discover.

Unfortunately, although all religions in the world are well intended, they fall short of the mark simply because they go against the core nature of the Divine, which is freedom of the Spirit. All rites are, in a way, limiting the greatness of the Divine. The more restrictive and circumscribed a belief is, the further away one is from understanding the Truth. Suppose you want to fulfill your divine purpose and experience the powers within the core of human existence. In that case, you must do away from all doctrines and focus solely on achieving three levels of integrity.

Integrity is the pillar of all virtues and the key to uncovering our Light Being. The first level is straightforward: "*Keeping your word.*" Unsurprisingly, this first step eliminates a large segment of people before they start the journey. If you strive for progress on this path, there's no place for dishonesty. Honoring your commitments is the first step towards awakening your co-creative powers.

The second level, closely related to the first yet fundamentally different, involves honoring your feelings and emotions: "*Acting consistent with your feelings.*" This means aligning your actions with your emotions and allowing yourself to fully experience a spectrum of emotions that arise in your life until you reach a position of detached observation rather than being subsumed by the experience.

Finally, when you have mastered these preliminary levels of integrity, you begin the most challenging level: "*Behaving consistently with your true self*." The best way to understand this is to recognize that as your awareness broadens, so does your understanding of your identity. Each new chapter in the narrative of your life offers lessons that reveal a fresh perspective, collectively forming the mosaic of your Being. Every part of you - your pain, trauma, victories, losses, emotional growth, physiological and spiritual developments, and setbacks - must be acknowledged. These are integrated into your newly formed behavioral framework and must be respected. Once you let go of the desire to label and categorize, you will start to navigate freely as you were Divinely designed right from the beginning.

However, it's not an easy path. Many succumb to the challenges, ignore their inner callings, or numb their pain with material distractions, from indulgence in vices to dependence on psychological barriers, psychoactive substances, or prescription medication. The list goes on.

If we were all honest with each other and recognized that the material aspects of life are not the answers, we could strive to make the world a better place. Unfortunately, the socioeconomic system is built upon numerous falsehoods, the most pervasive of which suggests that through excessive consumption of exogenous items, we will somehow experience lasting happiness. Regardless of who you are, this perceived state of joy is always temporary and tends to incite more of the same seeking. If we all understood that the true nature of reality is nothing more than a game of hide and seek within ourselves, we would continue to strive for more significant achievements. Indeed, we would inhabit a different paradigm that could mitigate unnecessary suffering. As I elaborated in a previous letter, while pain is inevitable, sustained suffering, a state of disassociation with our Higher Being, is avoidable.

Back to where we started, the best things in life happen when we are not looking. I can't count all the instances when I asked the Divine for a specific outcome in my life only to encounter the opposite. I was always left with incomplete parts of a giant puzzle, with pieces that didn't fit together, questioning whether anyone was even listening to my prayers. Little did I understand that they were being perfectly answered. The understanding of this entire video game, simulation, 3D environment, 'Matrix,' or whatever you prefer, is this: *"You don't always get what you want; instead, you certainly always receive what you need"* to BECOME what you desire. We are Human BEINGS, not Human DOINGS, right? Therefore, that which you seek is seeking embodiment within you.

For example, you might wonder why no good people seem to remain in this world or when you will meet the love of your life that is a perfect match, etc. Indeed, the Universe might conspire for decades until one day, you realize that YOU ARE the person you've been seeking. Until you genuinely embrace BEING the best human, you will face unpleasant experiences that teach you how NOT to act. In other words, you will encounter as many deceptive or hurtful people as necessary until you understand how NOT to present yourself to the world, enabling you to become the most LOVING person on earth. It's like magic when you consciously decide to embody a state of BEING that resonates with your desired fulfillment. Suddenly, you'll find yourself surrounded by the people you initially sought. The irony is that our Heavenly Father, in his sarcastic humor, presents us with what we desire only once we've stopped searching because we've BECOME it. The material world reflects our inner state, so stop chasing others or the material aspects of your life and concentrate on your inner Being. Evaluate yourself honestly, understanding who you are and how that reflects what you seek to attract. Then, release the wish, knowing wholeheartedly that if it is meant for you, it will find you once you evolve into the person who naturally aligns with the fulfillment of that wish. This is the missing key in the famous movie and book, 'The Secret.' To conquer this game on all its levels, you don't need anything beyond what you were naturally equipped with at birth.

Remember, base your entire existence on each level of integrity, surrender, accept, love unconditionally, and expect the Magic to happen because it will.

Sacred Medicines

An Instrument, Not an Endpoint – The Wounded Healer Syndrome

As my life was utterly unraveling once again, unbeknownst to me then, it was the beginning of what many would call "*my dark night of the soul.*" In August 2019, I faced my deepest shadows and childhood wounds and had a decision to make. Either I would continue going my own way for the rest of my life with blinders on, or what is customary in my journey would be to confront the issues head-on and prevail. Losing the love of my life had left me emotionally paralyzed, and the will to live had abandoned me. I had given everything of myself and my soul to have a family, and no matter how hard I tried, I was not getting back from life the love and self-acceptance so desperately needed. Confronted with suicidal thoughts, I sought help in psychoanalysis and quickly realized that, in my case, it was a lost cause and a complete waste of time and money. The pain I was feeling inside my chest was so pervasive and intense that it completely obscured my existence. I could not work, and it was even hard to breathe; it needed to be gone, or soon I would be gone.

That is when something inside me started to whisper, and inspiration arrived in tiny steps. First, it began with a forty-day fast-mimicking diet during which I limited my calories to less than five hundred per day. I started meditating, and during these early days, I would get "downloads" of complete applied wisdom. It was truly magical; my awareness of both the world, as I thought it was, and myself began to expand before my eyes. Something I couldn't understand or pinpoint was guiding my healing. I remember different people entering my life, from Reiki healers with extraordinary abilities to enlightened souls whom I didn't know then; they had participated in sacred ceremonies and knew that this reality has more secrets than the ones that meet the eye. During these days, the Spirit whispered during two meditations in the early morning hours. First, "*Stop eating all animal products.*" And the following week, "*Get out of all social media.*" True to my persona, I complied immediately when I got guidance from the ethereal, as by then, I knew better than not to.

As the pain would not subside, I was willing to do anything to be able to heal my broken heart, even if it could cost me my life. Someone suggested that I experiment with a psilocybin mushroom ceremony to try to stop the pain. Up until that day in my life, I had never done anything that could be considered a "drug." So, the emotional and societal connotations of breaking with the identifications of what I was led to believe all my life were acceptable behaviors versus an unknown path utilizing what the government had designated a controlled substance were tremendous. Yet I had to muster the courage to face it head-on as everything else was not working. Albeit doing all the research and concluding that they were not addictive, I did not know the consequences or long-term side effects, if any. Today, I laugh as the only side effect is an awakened mind that can see through every lie ever told.

Nothing had prepared me to overcome such labels. I felt ashamed for trying alternative means to heal something that was broken within. I had played by the rules; I had complied with everything I was told I had to since childhood. Study, work hard, don't cheat, play by rules, give your best, love, marry, have a family, and act with integrity. I checked every box and gave it my all, but nobody told me the truth. The truth is that society was broken to the core, that we are all entangled in perpetuating a lie, that everyone is after taking from others what is not theirs to take. And to feel whole, we break everyone else in the process.

We call it "*just business*" as a disguise for the true meaning of cheating and stealing. Honor and integrity are more precious than gold today, but even more precious than this is unselfishness, a genuinely giving heart capable of providing for others with no self-aspirations. Both a blessing and a curse, giving hearts such as these are so rare that they can't conceive of imposing their selfish ways on others, as there is no selfishness in them. Hearts like these get torn to shreds in modern materialistic societal constructs because individuals such as me can't play by the low standards everyone else adheres to, including in interpersonal loving relationships. With such a heart and wholly torn to pieces, I had no choice but to dive into the pool's deep end and seek alternate solutions for uncommon situations. The first and second therapies didn't have much effect on me at all. I was left with no solutions to the gaping hole now consuming my every breath.

The Reiki healer suggested that I learn about Ayahuasca. Ayahuasca is a South American psychoactive brew traditionally used by indigenous cultures and folk healers in the Amazon and Orinoco basins for spiritual ceremonies, divination, and healing of a variety of psychosomatic complaints. I had never heard the word before; I googled as much information as possible over the weekend. It was not as common as it is today, and frankly, given the illegal connotation portrayed by the ever-expanding government oversight, I was petrified. Today, I understand that, knowingly or not, governments' sole mission is to perpetuate the system and avoid the emergence of independent thought, as the creation of free thinkers may jeopardize the status quo. Free people, with conscious, sobering divine authority and self-worth, do not settle for blind, silent obedience; we tend to be a nuisance on the sidelines.

It comes as no surprise that all these awareness-expanding medicines from nature are categorized under the same label as truly destructive substances like other lab-made synthetic, addictive drugs to curtail their utilization at all costs. The more I learned, the more curious I was to try; I knew that if any truth were hidden in plain sight, I would have to summon the courage to find out firsthand. I found a place in Iquitos, Peru, run by several Shipibo Indian shamans, that seemed legitimate enough to try. This tribe is well known for its relationship with the Amazon and the practice of these ceremonies. Nothing could have prepared me for the transformation I was about to experience. In my quest to know the truth, I needed to find out what was hidden behind these ancient traditions, as everything I had been taught so far in my life seemed to be a lie. I couldn't continue living in a way that was against my nature. My Spirit was screaming to be shown to me.

There I was only a week after I resolved to leave my old self behind, disembarking on a September afternoon in 2019 in Iquitos. After a short twenty-kilometer drive into the outskirts of town and later a few more into the jungle through a dirt road, I arrived at a compound with a few thatch huts and very modest but nice bungalows with metal tin roofs. I said, wow, what a contrast from Southeast Florida. The property seemed to be a bubble surrounded by an almost pristine nature. I was shown to the orientation in a common area hut, where I met a few participants already in their second or third week in the program. Everyone seemed to be friendly and had a different shine to their eyes. I was still all wound up, wounded, and closed in a defensive posture, not knowing what to expect. Two days before my first ceremony, I had to acclimate and destress. Nothing could have prepared me for what would happen during the next two weeks. As is customary with me, if I am going to do something, I go all in, not halfway. So, I signed up for what is called a *"plant diet,"* an intense two-week eight-ceremony program that was supposed to heal my broken heart.

Through a healthy natural diet that does not include sugar, caffeine, and salt, the body gets ready to open a gateway into other dimensions of consciousness. I will not openly share my experiences because everyone gets what is needed in their journeys. If I predispose you with mine, it is simply a selfish act to boast my ego and serves no other purpose than to say hey, look at me, how great I am, and this is not the intent of this share. I have openly shared some but never all of these insights with other brothers and sisters who have common elements in their journeys to mine when appropriate. But to summarize, the experiences were more than revealing; I got to know the true nature of myself, nature, and the universe, life after death, and both the release of the old and the healing of my identity began.

These ceremonies are not for everyone and certainly not for the faint of heart. It will take a lot of self-determination to see them through, integrate the wisdom attained later, and do the inner work. But each ceremony is the equivalent of over twenty to thirty years of psychotherapy, in my opinion. In my opinion, it is even better because it attacks the root cause of mental distress or post-traumatic disorders by rewiring the neural pathways of the brain. Throughout these ceremonies, I freed myself from most childhood wounds and identifications. It was not an easy process, but a complimentary one to my spiritual journey.

A word of caution: I've seen many participating in over 20 to 100 ceremonies, and I don't judge or begrudge anyone's journeys. However, some end up caught in an escape loop where they use these ceremonies to cope instead of as a stepping tool to overcome a stage in their development. One needs to recognize this and muster the courage to confront the wreckage of the prior reality and mold it into submission by accepting and releasing it.

Would I do it all over again, knowing what I know today? Yes, I would, as these tools provided me with a shortcut to the core of my being. They enabled me to free myself quickly from prior identifications and lighten the load on my shoulders. They also allowed me to empathize even more with others who have gone or are going through similar lessons in their lives. This enables me to be of greater service in their journeys and shed some light and hope on potential psychological and emotional traps they may be in.

How do we change the world? One soul at a time. Never underestimate the power of the compounding effect.

The Act of Renunciation

Embracing the Gift yet to come

As I shared in the previous chapters, the Spirit had manifested. I had accepted the renunciation of my old emotional attachments and, with this, the identity that needed to die off so the new one could be born. As the last two weeks of December went on, I made the conscious decision to show up in the lives of those I was leaving behind as the best version of myself. I said to myself with every warm embrace I gave, "*This is what unconditional love is and what a father, lover, boyfriend, brother, mother, father... etc., should do. Thank you for showing up in my life to teach me the lessons you did; you are now free. I know who you are in Truth.*" I gave my best in every aspect of these interactions, knowing that each of the souls that had appeared until that day in my life did so in common accord to experience these lessons alongside me. Nothing but acceptance and a heightened sense of peace permeated my existence. As the holidays passed, it was time to say goodbye and leave.

In these heightened states of awareness, I had begun months ago to soften the emotional blow I was about to take by the end of the year. I started reaching out to other people and trying to meet individuals who might also be going through their awakening journey. Fortunately, I met an extraordinary person online. I didn't know then how important this person was about to become in my journey or that we even had a prior connection from a previous timeline. To summon the courage and raise my expectations for what was to come, I spontaneously agreed to meet this person in her native country during the first eight days of 2023. I figured I wasn't ready for anything new to enter my life yet, but I wanted to continue making sense of the journey I had agreed to undertake.

Throughout our interactions before my visit, we discovered that the Spirit had begun showing up in our lives approximately simultaneously. In her case, she had undergone a very similar process of purging the old to embrace the new, and I was eager to compare notes face to face. I couldn't wait. So off I went, and during what can only be categorized as a magical first few days, we got in touch with nature and experienced a simpler life than the one we often live in modern society. We exchanged our spiritual gifts with each other. Hours turned into full-day discussions about our manifestations and the implications for the lives we were to lead.

As I explained earlier, each soul entering our lives comes for an exchange. We both learn from each other and serve as mirrors for the benefit of our evolution. I'll only share a few critical aspects of our exchange since it's the example rather than the content that matters. In my case, I had gained the gnostic knowledge of what a Natural Diet was, which she also needed to acquire. I've dedicated a whole chapter to this information, so that I won't go into much detail here. So, during those days, I shared my insights and instructed her on my adopted methods. In her way, she also reciprocated with the wisdom she had gained.

You might ask, what's so special about that? Nothing extraordinary, right? Hold that thought before you jump to any conclusions. Halfway through the week, coincidentally, we did a big grocery haul at an excellent supermarket on a Wednesday at noon. At that moment, Spirit spoke to her as I was about to pay for the purchases. From what I recall, she later shared that she felt the usual presence of Spirit and heard the words, *"Heal Him."* A quick side note: you never get highly detailed instructions from the Spirit. At that moment, she was inclined to place her hand over my right shoulder as I faced her and the cashier.

I will try to describe what happened next, but I may not do it justice. What could be described as a supernatural vision unfolded in my mind? Some might call it an activation of our third eye or others of our pineal gland. Either way, no one can confirm these gifts or how they come about, but many can attest to the human ability to have visions as vivid as the reality we perceive through sight. At that moment, with the palpable sensation of it occurring in real-time, I saw a white light enter my body from the back, passing between all my organs and muscles. It was almost like seeing a live MRI scan in my head. This light reached and encircled my heart, and I felt my heart instantly jolt within my chest cavity, seemingly shifting its position. I can't determine what exactly changed or was healed. What I can confirm is that after this event, many of my past hurts from failed emotional relationships seemed to fade away from my consciousness and memory. It was as if Spirit had performed a master emotional reset of my "hard drive" containing that information. I was free once again, but I didn't realize it then.

Completely stunned and frozen for what must have been a few minutes, the cashier asked me if I was okay. As the vision left me and I regained my breath, I responded, yes, everything is alright. I paid for our groceries and then turned to my friend, asking her what on earth had happened. I was met by the sparkle of kind eyes and a warm smile there.

Once we both got back in the car and everything settled, we shared what we felt and experienced. It was like mutual reassurance that we weren't going mad and on an extraordinary journey. As the week went on, we continued our exchanges and revelations. She disclosed that she had met me in a past life but didn't share anything more than that. We agreed to stay in touch and see where life would take us next, with a sense of adventure and awe akin to children playing freely in a playground.

As we said our farewells, I remember feeling complete peace that day. I had a hotel reservation near the airport but stayed at an airport capsule hotel to avoid the early morning rush hour. What happened next was something I could never have anticipated. I was awakened by a bright light, similar to my past experiences, but it was distinctly different this time. I could barely see anything in the room, only the bed I was lying on and the outlines of the room through my peripheral vision amidst an all-encompassing light. During this, I felt the same unconditional divine love I'd initially encountered in my vivid dream about my grandfather, Oscar. Almost as if I was about to pass to the other side. Yet, I heard a mighty voice stating, *"I have come to wake you up so you finally understand that I am you, and you are me."* Unable to see anything but a beautiful three-dimensional lotus flower-like apparition turning on itself and the engulfing light, I reached to touch the flower. I passed out as the energy was too great.

Later, I learned that the lotus flower is widely recognized for its symbolic meanings of purity, spiritual awakening, rebirth, and overcoming adversity. It grows in muddy waters and rises above the surface to bloom with remarkable beauty. The lotus flower's ability to emerge clean and pristine from murky waters each day is often seen as a metaphor for the human spirit's capacity to remain untouched by the impurities of the environment. It rises above worldly attachments and ignorance. The "turning on itself" describes the lotus flower's daily cycle of closing at night and reopening with the sunrise. This cycle can symbolize rebirth or renewal, as the lotus flower perpetually renews itself daily. It could also represent introspection or self-reflection, as the flower's closing might be seen as a turning inward and its opening as an expression of awakening and enlightenment. It was a strong message from beyond that I had achieved a spiritual victory in my life's journey and entered a new chapter or stage.

That morning, I woke up in time to catch my flight. Despite the incomprehensibility of what had transpired just a few hours earlier, I checked in and boarded my plane. It took me the rest of the year to integrate these events into my understanding and even longer to gather the courage to share them with loved ones and the world.

As we progress on the path of truth, it becomes easier to tread, as our true selves fear nothing more than inauthenticity.

The final lesson in this passage is the realization that we are one and the same, experiencing reality through our senses, but at our core, as I've mentioned before, we are divine. Our bodies are temples that deserve honor and respect. I hope to share these experiences to encourage a questioning of the lies you may have been told throughout your life and inspire your journey of discovery for the benefit of all.

Navigating Towards Choiceless Observation

In Pursuit of Inner Equilibrium: The Power of Amicable Stillness

I had just come from my trip in early January of 2023 and had experienced the miraculous and most profound divine apparitions. I was destined to travel to Tamarindo, Costa Rica, on a sort of *"Eat, Pray, Love"* trip with the intent to continue my inner journey. I was supposed to meet a dear friend there to accompany me during those days, but she couldn't make it at the last minute and had to cancel the trip while she was already at the airport. I was very disappointed and almost considered returning to Miami, as I had no idea what I would do there by myself, not knowing anyone.

While there, the energy and vibe differed from what I had anticipated. The laid-back feel of the surroundings allowed me to let my guard down and continue experiencing more *"downloads"* as I was uncertain about what to expect next. During the few days I was there, the Divine started to show me that I was not alone in my awakening journey and that the Universe was conspiring for me to reach the right people at the right place and time.

I was at the Mother Earth Vegan Hotel on the first night, contemplating returning the following day, when the magic started as usual. I woke up with an intense feeling of peace. I looked at the clock, and it was 1:21 AM, and the spirit spoke, "*You are not leaving here as you have things to do here.*" I acknowledged the message and remained grateful for the guidance. With this new insight, I embraced the morning and set out to seize the day. Every day for the next five days, I randomly stumbled upon enlightened beings who opened up and passionately shared their journeys with me. This reaffirmed that I was not alone in this quest and, most importantly, that my perceived craziness was, in fact, a sign of returning to our essence.

Again, concerning the anonymity of the encounters, I will change the names and the exchanges, but I want to drive the point that once we establish the link with the Divine within, our lives take a turn for the better. It will not always be painless either; many times, it will be utterly painful as we detach from our egos and aspects of the old self, which are pretty lodged in our subconscious and tend to bring the most significant challenges but also the most prominent lessons and opportunities for change on how we show up in the world later.

As I was returning from having the best time ever meeting my new Venezuelan surfing instructor, a "Chama" with whom I connected immediately gave her a beautiful soul. If you read my prior chapters, you will understand the irony that Spirit is bringing another Venezuelan to make up for what the previous one did in my life. Anyways, back to that timeline. I was entering the hotel when a gentleman, with whom we later became lovely friends, blocked my way and forcefully introduced himself as the hotel manager. For a minute, I thought something terrible had happened or that I was, in fact, in some sort of trouble, although unbeknown to me. Within the third sentence coming out of his mouth, he probably realized by the look on my face that I was a bit taken back, and he stated, *"No worries, everything is alright; I just want to invite you to a communal dinner tonight here at the hotel, we have an Argentine Chef visiting and thought you would appreciate it!"* More magic, as again, alone and with no plans, the Universe started taking care of me. Little would I know what was in store for me. Dinner time came, and a long table with over a dozen participants was there. I sat in the middle and started socializing. Right before me was a couple from Canada I had never seen before. As we started talking, I quickly learned that we had a lot in common; we had all done Ayahuasca ceremonies, and we were well on our way to experiencing a different relationship with the reality surrounding us. As the minutes turned into hours of a delightful dinner with excellent, unique culinary creations and enriching conversations, I couldn't help noticing a necklace the couple's wife sitting right across was wearing. I had never been so captured by a stone, let alone a Tigers Eye mounted on what seemed to be an eagle. Yet I felt as if it was calling me. Little did I know the creator behind the pendent, its significance, and who had ward it before her. As the night went on, I chose to stop staring at the pendant before anyone would notice me.

The following day, as I was going for breakfast by the hotel's pool, my new Canadian friends were sitting there and invited me to join them. What started at ten in the morning finished at two in the afternoon only because they needed to check out the hotel and head to their respective jobs at a famous retreat center. I am detailing such a lengthy interaction because what was about to happen that day was truly magical. As we shared our journeys and encounters with hidden truth, the voice of Spirit kept telling me, *"Give her your bracelets and tell her I say so."* I didn't want to. I had recently bought these beads, and I loved them. But the presence was persistent, and I had to interrupt my friend in the middle of one of her stories to tell her point-blank, *"Spirit is asking me to gift you my two bead bracelets, so here you go; they are significant to me."* She looked at me, her eyes watering, and said, *"Stay here. Don't go anywhere."* She ran upstairs to her room and back. To my surprise, she extended her hand to me, opened it, and there it was, the necklace from last night with the Tiger's Eye. She said, *"Spirit has been telling me to give it to you, but it's also a precious gift from a dear friend. I have been looking at your bracelet beads all morning and told myself I wanted some like them."* I told her this necklace had attracted my attention last night, and I couldn't take my eyes away from it. We proceeded with the exchange.

We were both moved by the power that was unfolding before us. Somehow, we were connected and guided, indicative of a divine intelligence that would lead us at every step if we surrendered, flowed, and remained open to our natural state. Looking back, I understand the message and lesson behind it all. Early Christians used to share their belongings; they lacked nothing in life. They lived in communes, and everyone worked to provide their share of labor for everyone's benefit. Our most cherished possessions mean nothing unless we can share them openly with one another, as nothing belongs to us long-term. We are all passing pilgrims in this land. And yes, I advocate for private property rights, but that is not the point I am driving here. We can only truly experience something when we share with those who reciprocate and openly share with us. Living alone in a seven-bedroom luxury estate only works well if you have loved ones to fill those empty rooms. Yet I bemusedly observe wealthy individuals who buy such mansions to live alone. What is the point?

How bereft of self-worth must one be to amass an excessive amount of wealth and flaunt it through not one, but sometimes up to four or six such properties, which most of the time sit empty or are occupied solely by them. Perhaps the examples of my great-grandfather and grandfather who reached these heights influenced me. I recall their properties hosting numerous visitors — we were a large family. Such estates were the venues for fantastic get-togethers almost every weekend during my childhood summers. For the longest time, I have aspired to recreate such a place here in the U.S. so that my closest friends and visiting family could experience the same joys of my childhood. Unfortunately, circumstances have not yet permitted such events. Given the direction in which our society is heading, I feel more inclined to recreate this oasis somewhere else in the world where higher moral values still prevail.

Back to the necklace story, we were like two little children visited by their Father with new gifts, giggling at the perfection of the event. She called her friend the artist who had created the necklace, and she had a fascinating life story and spiritual journey. Coincidentally, she happened to be in town only for that day, and we proceeded to arrange a face-to-face meeting with me that afternoon, as she was curious to get to know the story behind the man that her necklace chose as a new host. So, there, in one short sweep by Spirit, I made new like-minded friends, and my social agenda was filled to the rim, creating new, lasting, meaningful relationships. The best things always come when we least expect them and remain open to the unknown.

But the magic of these early days in communion with the Spirit was not nearly over. More people, circumstances, and coincidences occurred during the next few days. As I was prepared to conquer this new level of the simulation, I was provided with the proper game tools. The most profound exchanges happened the following day, also by the hotel pool as I was sunbathing. As I commune with the Angel of the Sun, as I like to call it, I receive a vast, profound exchange with Spirit via a presential download. I felt a pleasant ecstasy, as is customary when Spirit is present, and my awareness heightened to supernatural levels. In this surreal stillness, I heard, *"You have reached these levels of enlightenment in prior lives; you failed then because your ego got in the way of your powers. This time, you must become a Choiceless Observer and Sit Still."* Oh boy, was I in for a rude awakening of the totality of implications of this revelation in later parts of the game?

See, there is a catch to this game; imagine a game of soccer where you have two 45-minute periods. In the first half of the match, you're winning by a high margin. The game is in your favor, and you say, *"Piece of cake; I have this game made."* Only to come out during the second half and discover that your adversaries not only had learned your every weakness over the first period but now have taken steroids and are twice as strong and fast, kicking your rear end. Well, that is how this Spiritual game works: every time we reach a new level of awareness and communion, we are greeted with welcome gifts and laurels, and then, as in a perfect closed circle, the other half of the level, we are put into a test to see if we truly learned anything or not. It is a trial by fire to determine if we are ready for the next level in a never-ending cycle of expansion until we fully develop and are released by Grace into our highest awareness, Christ's Consciousness. In this state, we fully express our Divine Being in communion with Divinity, like Jesus Christ, Buddha, Mohammed, etc. Now, there is no obligation to pass any level, and we are free to stay and call it quits at any point. But for some of us who had pre-existing soul agreements, we are called to the opportunity to keep going further along the path in one lifetime. And as you can imagine, I have never turned down the chance of a great adventure. What the heck, I am giving it a fair shot! The question is, why wouldn't you want to know what your maximum potential looks like? That is the dare I made to myself some time ago. I reasoned that our Heavenly Father has a master plan for my many lives and that the only thing between reality and that outcome had to be me. So, I decided to follow the instructional manual provided this time around.

I am becoming a choiceless observer and sitting still!

Embracing the Divine

An Exploration into the Emotional Healing of Others

For the longest time, I wanted to have the opportunity to travel to Europe, like what my grandfather, Oscar, once did. Rent a car and drive through each country to experience the cultures and the people. Get in touch with other aspects of life besides the mere monotonous everyday existence. Depending on what kind of individual you are, you can think of my life as a glass that is half empty or half full. The truth, as I explained, is truly subjective. I had millions, and I had nothing, and frankly, I consider myself extremely lucky and blessed through each one of these cycles of creation and destruction. When I take inventory, I lived a life full of experiences that have been more than the life of an average individual. Each stage gets shorter and shorter as I detach and grow in my conscious awareness and allow the Divine to commune with me in my everyday life.

It was the beginning of 2023 when I met my new girlfriend, and we decided to take an open-ended trip through Europe, a lifelong dream of mine. We drove over 6,500 kilometers and visited 130 cities in France, where half of my family is descended from, while the other half is of Spanish and Italian descent. We were then invited to the most beautiful wedding I had ever attended, hosted in Greece by two of our dear soul family friends. While in Greece, we let loose and enjoyed the food and drinks, though still no animal flesh for me, as my body no longer allows it. People often ask me when the last time I ate meat was, and that was six months after the beginning of my awakening at a barbecue "*parrillada*" my brother hosted at his house in Argentina. I vividly remember it; my brother went all out and bought the best meat available, which everyone else deemed delicious but me. My taste buds were thus clean by then, and I could smell the rot in the flesh and feel the dead energy in the meat. I was only able to have a few bites before my stomach started to protest, and excruciating spasms ensued, making it impossible for me to eat anymore. These days, when I want to indulge, I enjoy various types of cheese, eggs in the form of pastries or desserts, and bread with wine; who in their right mind would say no to French patisseries? But even these foods temporarily disconnect me from my heightened conscious awareness. Henceforth, I only indulge in cultural exploration for brief periods lasting less than a few days. I bring these details up for several reasons. My book will provoke many readers to judge and criticize my persona, which is expected but unfair. Some will brush off my anecdotes as a defense mechanism to avoid feeling inadequate or confronting their existence. Others will immediately start looking for ways to discredit me, which is also alright. I do not fear criticism or judgment. After all, nobody can destroy who I've become; I have nothing to hide, and my transparency is unwavering. I am quick to admit all my flaws, inadequacies, and failures. I do not conform to the world's rules anymore, and if you have yet to notice, I only answer to a Higher Law than the ones we are force-fed. I want to be clear: I am an imperfect human. If there is one claim to fame, I accept that it's being recognized as a truth seeker. In my relentless quest to discover the ultimate truths, I realized that all truth is subjective as it is observed through the senses, which filter over 80% of the information, if not more, considering the observer's emotional state. But as I delved deeper, I discovered the Divine as the sole, absolute Truth behind the tapestry of reality.

Returning to Greece after an amazing four weeks traveling through France and an enjoyable first week in Greece with friends, we knew it was time to slow down and detox. I can only immerse myself so much in worldly activities before feeling the need to reconnect with nature and return to more natural eating habits, such as fasting and consuming raw fruits and vegetables. Thus, we briefly retreated to FZeen Resort in Cephalonia, Ionian Islands in Greece. This week, I asked my girlfriend for some solitude, dedicating my time to introspection through morning meditations and contemplation amidst some of the most beautiful pine trees. The turquoise translucent waters of the Ionian Sea are unique.

Greek culture is fantastic; people understand what is essential in life beyond materialism.

During one of these days at the resort, after mainly eating fruit, I noticed the presence of an extraordinary soul. Allow me to digress here for a minute so you can understand the points I will be making shortly. First, it is never me doing anything related to the emotional healing of others; the only thing I do is get out of the way of the Spirit. This means I empty myself of all my identity and thoughts; I sit still and allow whatever words or energy come through me to take over. If that makes sense, it is almost like I am a passenger in my body.

I was overlooking the beautiful ocean in the open-air gym at the resort, walking on the treadmill surrounded by other people, including many beautiful women. But I couldn't care less about the activities around me, and I mentioned this because of what would happen. You must understand my frame of mind; otherwise, you may misconstrue the point. As I was taken by the beauty of the surroundings and view, I felt a presence, and there was this charming younger woman in her mid-thirties walking amidst the garden toward the gym. Generally, I am extra cautious when it comes to Spiritual guidance, and I have made a deal with our Heavenly Father; I will act once I am provided with physical presential evidence that I am being called to the stage. Soon, you will know the meaning of one of the embossed symbols in this book, which I have kept secret from you thus far. As this presence caught my attention and made me notice the soul walking past me, I said, *"If there is something I need to do here, it will be shown to me."* I lowered my gaze and kept exercising. The day went normal;

my girlfriend was taking her classes, and I decided to go down to town by the mountainside and explore the ocean to reconnect with nature. That afternoon, I went to buy some more fruit, and as I was coming into the resort, out of the blue, this young lady I mentioned earlier literally jumped in front of me in the garden trail out of nowhere. Again, I felt the presence of her soul, and I said to myself once again the same thing as in that prior morning at the gym, lowering my gaze and minding my own.

Generally, I am not the kind to go to group meditation sessions. However, I resolved that year that although I had been shown the Divine already, I would allow myself to explore everything others did to relate better. I decided that on September 8th, I would like to sign up for a meditation class at 7:00 pm. As I arrived, I met the same woman who I had twice encountered that day and not spoken to as the instructor. I giggled, smiled, and introduced myself, to which she told me, *"Nice to meet you; everyone else canceled, so I guess I am spending my birthday with you ..."* I immediately felt bad for her since I have spent many of my birthdays alone or in suboptimal occasions, in particular, my fiftieth birthday was probably one of the very worst days of my life till now as I received the physical verification that I needed to renounce to my prior life emotional attachments and that I had been living an illusion till that very day. So, being the empath that I am, I suggested canceling as well, to which she disagreed as she had no other plans than to spend that night alone with her cat at home.

Given that I had already felt her soul presence, I knew that Spirit was cooking something, but I did not want to jump to any conclusions; I told her, *"I may have a birthday present for you, but I need a sign."* She looked at me funny and asked me what I was talking about, to which I quickly answered never mind what I said. Spirit had something planned for her and me that I will never forget, primarily because September 8th is also the birthday of my oldest stepdaughter, whom I adopted as my own, albeit the mother taking them away from me. My daughter once told me when she was little, *"You are a miracle in my life."* But that is another story amongst the many that I will keep for myself.

Back that night, during the meditation class, this woman spoke about self-love and unconditional love. I gnostically know this lesson: I was smiling with my eyes closed when I connected with the Ethereal, and I said to Spirit... *"Listen, I am not being of service until you show yourself to me and give me a clear sign that you want to use me. This woman knows my girlfriend, and I am not acting weird here unless you want me to..."*.

Little had prepared me for what happened next; I immediately asked for a sign and my secret call to the stage code, and I was there. As I like to call it, *"You are not imagining any of this"* showed up with a repeating bang. As I kept hearing what seemed to me like a loud knocking by my side, I was forced to open my eyes and draw my attention to a dragonfly, my Spirit animal, knocking against the window from the inside right on top of the head of the instructor. I once again giggled, and the minute I was aware of the dragonfly, it stopped, flipping its wings in place.

The instructor finished the meditation at 8:00 pm on September 8th; there is also a hidden meaning behind the number eight for those who know you will understand. I approached her and said, *"I got my sign. Could we speak some more?"* I emptied myself to create the space between us for open-heart sharing and allow Spirit to take over. If you recall reading prior chapters, our souls are like tuning forks; once we attain a higher frequency in our awareness, we are constantly capable of resonating at these frequencies, and if we keep a clean temple, the Spirit does the rest for us, we just be ourselves, and everything happens around us for us. In this case, I remember sharing my lessons of self-love and unconditional love as a means for her healing, which she was, in a way, going through the same lessons in her soul's journey. At one point in our conversation, my girlfriend showed up to pick me up, and we all three walked under the beautiful night sky littered with billions of stars. We all proceeded then to call it a night and did not think much of it.

Nothing could have prepared me for what happened the following day. My girlfriend and I attended another stretching class in the garden, and there she was, the same lady from the day before acting as the instructor. By then, I was *"connected,"* having just finished my morning meditation under some of my favorite pine trees overlooking the turquoise ocean. If I were to choose my idea of heaven for the first few weeks, I would replicate the shoreline of the Ionian

Sea. She approached me and told me that the words I had spoken the previous night had moved her profoundly, so much so that she began her emotional healing and journey to self-love. Again, due to confidentiality, I will never openly share personal details of the events; frankly, they are not the point. We are all here to help each other and be of service if we allow ourselves the opportunity instead of solely focusing on what I like to call the "*little me*," our egos.

I assumed that was that, and we proceeded with the class. As we were saying our goodbyes, the instructor started asking about my experiences in Iquitos, Peru, with the Shipibo Shamans. While sharing my experiences, I found myself genuinely gazing into her eyes. Not many can withstand my penetrating stare. To me, eyes are the doorway to the soul, and sometimes, I can see auras or even past lives if I concentrate long enough. But this time, something completely unexpected occurred, an event that I'd never experienced before or since. As I gazed into this woman's soul, I had an instantaneous out-of-body supernatural experience. My consciousness connected to the universe's core, where the Divine resides. There, I felt the presence of the Divine, and within milliseconds, I was returned to the 3D simulation— in a journey long enough for me to be aware of the unfolding magic and that I was simply along for the ride. As a faithful servant, my only role was to remain empty and not interfere with the healing process. Back in reality, I felt the same energy in my chest as during the demon encounter or that January morning at the airport hotel. Just as my chest felt ready to burst, a wave of energy left me and moved towards her. The second the energy hit her, this woman's eyes shook side to side, her body trembled, and she gasped for air. We stood still; she looked at me, puzzled by what had happened, and said, "*You felt me!*"

I don't like drawing attention to myself; hence, I downplayed the entire event, unsure of what had precisely occurred since it was the first time that Spirit had acted in such a way through me. I didn't know what to say. I responded, "*Yeah, I felt something myself,*" she replied, "*I don't know when and where, but I'm sure we'll meet again...*" To my surprise, two weeks later, my girlfriend received a text message from her. She said meeting both of us was the best birthday gift the universe had ever given her and that she had discovered Self-Love within herself. At that moment, I understood that Spirit had used my soul again as a tuning fork to attune this lady's soul. I had already learned this lesson in the simulation, and she was also ready to master that level by an act of Grace.

That same day, around midday, I looked for my girlfriend right after another gym class she had attended. She conversed with another instructor as I approached and was also working with her spiritual magic. I was, as I described it, running high in awareness. When I approached them, my girlfriend introduced me. Unexpectedly, Spirit delivered a message to this other woman, who promptly began to sob and explained that she felt something in her chest. I held her hand and reassured her while delivering the message. By the end of that day, my selflessness allowed me to help two sisters ascend to the next level in their journeys. Nothing is more rewarding than knowing I made a positive impact, especially when the Spirit chooses me to facilitate emotional healing.

The days went by uneventfully until the following week. One of my dreams has always been to buy a sailboat or catamaran and travel worldwide for a few years. We had chartered a catamaran for a journey through Zakynthos, also in the Ionian Sea, showcasing some of the most breathtaking scenery I've ever encountered. During my weeklong trip, I continued to immerse myself in nature and feed on only raw, fresh produce and fruits, complemented by a bit of sweet Greek wine, local honey, and Italian espresso. You could say I was in heaven, and as it turned out, I was about to experience a Divine gift that is still hard to comprehend. On the sixth day, in the middle of the ocean between two Ionian Islands, I felt the presence of Spirit again, but this time it was profoundly different. A dragonfly appeared out of nowhere - a rarity, considering none had been seen during the trip, and we were in the ocean. My girlfriend sitting by my side also noticed it, just in case you think I imagine things.

A side note for those who do not know: The dragonfly has deep spiritual meaning and symbolism across many cultures. It symbolizes transformation, self-realization, and spiritual growth. As a creature that undergoes a dramatic metamorphosis from an aquatic nymph to a flying adult, the dragonfly represents the ability to embrace changes and gain wisdom from facing challenges. In many cultures, the dragonfly is seen as a link between the earthly and spiritual realms, encouraging an exploration of the deeper aspects of one's existence and spiritual journey. The dragonfly's iridescent wings are also associated with shedding illusions and gaining clarity of vision. Dragonflies are considered a good omen, symbolizing positive changes, visits from spirits, opportunity, and self-realization. They are revered in Native American cultures for their transformative, healing, and protective qualities. The dragonfly is a powerful spiritual symbol representing transformation, self-discovery, living in the present moment, and connecting to the divine. How appropriate is it that Spirit has chosen this animal to show me when I am in its presence to ensure I do not doubt what is happening. I have had many such occasions in the past few years, but I will tell you only a few.

Let me express that the number 8 represents abundance, prosperity, balance, harmony, and infinite potential in numerology. Eight is associated with new beginnings, transformation, and going beyond the natural order. It symbolizes the divine, the supernatural, and transcending limitations. In the Bible, the number 8 is connected to salvation, resurrection, and God's intervention. It represents a fresh start and deliverance. Seeing the number 8 or 888 is a sign from angels to have faith, manifest abundance, and empower others. It encourages bold choices and aligning with one's true purpose. Spiritually, the number 8 signifies moving from perfection achievable through natural means (represented by the number 7) to a higher, supernatural state of being.

In summary, the number 8 holds deep spiritual significance across many traditions, representing themes of transformation, abundance, divine connection, and transcendence of limitations. I had my fair share of encounters with the number seven and later eight. Remember, the encounter with the Divine in the hotel was on January 8th, 2023.

As the dragonfly flew over me for a few minutes, my consciousness elevated to an unprecedented peak. In what felt like an eternity, I was experiencing unity with all of creation; it was as though the veil of reality had lifted, and my amnesia was temporarily cured. I remembered who I was and my purpose on earth. I recognized that my core being was not human; my essence was a fragment of the Divine. Consequently, everything around me was indeed an extension of me. The entire Kingdom was me; I had crossed the threshold of the Kingdom of Heaven on Earth for the first time in this lifetime. While fully conscious, I experienced the Christ within me; I understood beyond a doubt that the Heavenly Father and I were one in a gnostic sense. Over two hundred days have passed since that event and until the writing of this passage. These encounters have been the catalyst that led me to change the course of my life. I can't, in clear conscience, withhold this journey from others who might be prepared to experience a higher version of themselves.

I understand you are comfortable where you are today because it's familiar. But wouldn't you dare confront the unknown and accept discomfort to truly experience communion with the Spirit through your higher self? Imagine what you may be missing and awaiting to become!

Embracing Our Inborn Identity

The Journey towards Fulfilling Our Destiny

Who are we meant to become in this lifetime? Are we indeed allowed to become who we would like to be or who society expects us to be? Are our ego and its identifications the ultimate possible truth, or is it only one of the infinite ones? Are there some predestinated outcomes or experiences in our lives that we must endure, whether they are what we would have hoped for or not? What role does free will play in all of it, whether in luck or relationships?

Well, you are in for a treat because there is no one correct answer to them. I had my share of adventures in this incarnation, many resulting from my choices. Yet, the most pivotal ones were serendipitous, karmic, or predestined experiences that came about while facing utter dismay at the hand of my ego's blinding dictatorship, trying to comply with that life which was imposed on me since childhood where my two stern parents for lack of discernment obligated me to study and pursue a career that it was not my calling. I was molded into what they believed could give me the best footing in a middle-class society, but my passion or vocation was killed in the process. And I tell you if you want to experience hell, go to university for decades, and then end up in a soulless corporate job in America pursuing the so-called American Dream, which for many now has become the American Nightmare.

A human being's capacity for co-creating is proportionate to the passion instilled in its creation. You may try to force your way into fitting the mold, but yes, hard work and sweat will carry you through, and this has indeed worked for me for several decades. Even when I was laid off from my last corporate job, I somehow was forced into a professional intermediation role to attain my residence and be allowed to remain in the US rightfully. I was doing it to survive and comply with what was expected of me. Buy a house, marry, and have a family. The game's name always was, *I will feel fulfillment when this or that happens...* until then, I must lower my head and pull through; this is what society expects from me.

There is nothing more soul-clenching for anyone to be on a life path that is not what you were meant to be by Divine Design. Those of us who are faced with this predicament and are not strong enough commit suicide. I know first-hand accounts of close friends who took their lives in similar situations. I even contemplated this several times as my life's journey was never an easy one and mostly filled with loneliness and betrayal from everyone around me. A plant's fruit is only as juicy as the soil its seed has landed on; never underestimate the importance of being surrendered to the right environment if you would like to flourish.

Everyone tells you that work is supposed to suck, and that is why it is called work, or they may point to the opposite, which is not to settle until you find your passion. They would claim that experiencing it is as if you do not work one day of your life. Although both statements have truth and are diametrically opposing, they are the same: the message stems from the fact that one must sustain oneself through a forceful act. Yet, to my surprise, I discovered that I would only attain my financial or material objectives once I let go of them and surrendered. It was almost like a forcefield was opposing me every step of the way, and the intensity of the opposition was directly proportional to my striving. The harder I tried, the harder I would fail. Yet by an act of Grace, everything would fall into place when I did not drive my chariot but instead took a passenger seat. As any good scientist will attest, any experiment-derived conclusions by observation must be replicable. So, throughout my life, every time I reached what seemed to be a dead end, I reminded myself to let go of the reins of my life and take a passenger observant position while asking our Heavenly Father and his wisdom to take me to the next level of the game because I was stuck.

You probably wonder if this is nonsense and only applies to emotions or spiritual aspects, not the material. The whole of creation proved this assumption wrong; from several improbable outcomes, the right amount of capital or recourses would show up from seemingly nowhere. Everything that I was once striving for came to me when I stopped chasing it. If it was meant for me to experience it, I attracted it like a magnet and not through my ego's whims. So, the question remains: who controls what and why? This curious aspect of creation may or may not apply to others to the degree they are meant to experience it in their life journey and that which you signed up to experience. Everyone has a soul's plan, a master design we agree to come into our lives and experience. A curriculum of life circumstances that will allow us to attain the wisdom of the experiences that foster our ascension in the Spiritual realms.

Well, back to the prior point. My true passion differed from what I studied and ended up working on. My true passion was aviation; I did attain my certificates on my own accord and abilities, but I needed more financial support to make it a profession or a business. And my second one, architectural design, yet again, forcefully not allowed to pursue this either. As a professional, I was relegated to interior luxury renovations and luxury single-family development, where my job could have been more creative. Still, I had to police my business partner and employees to prevent them from stealing from me. Finally, when I was on top of a twenty-four-year pilgrimage, a former client, in collusion with another business partner, to which I extended all my resources to create one of my startups, stole everything from investors and me. This was the death blow of all my lifelong professional aspirations. It forced me to finally quit pushing the windmill stone up the mountain and rethink my identity and what I was meant to be. I couldn't continue having a spec of non-integrity in the tapestry of my life if I was to pass to the next level of mastery in the simulation. I had to do a *"CTRL+ALT+DEL"* of all the old software still running in the background of my subconscious mind, dictating the image of what success was meant to look like in this socioeconomic construct we all live in and by.

Knowing what I know today, I would have never walked the path I had chosen as a potentially viable outcome for my life. When I launched into the world back then, I had something to prove to those who had not seen me for who I was as a child, student, son, etc. The biggest drivers in my early years were the pain I carried inside me and the need to fill the void in my heart due to the upbringing I experienced.

Again, those were other days, but if you are a parent reading this, the enormous disservice you can do is to impose your views on your children about the need for a career or field of study. Let their Spirits show them the way. The good news is that no matter how far away one may have fallen from their true calling, Our Divine Father can do miracles after all. If we stop chasing our tails in pursuing material advancement and solely focus on discovering our inner gifts, we will naturally fit into the tapestry of this world. The value created will be proportional to our passion while building what is meant for us to be built. Our soul will shine through, and the Universe will conspire for us to be seen as who we were meant to become. Passion will be the driving force behind your creation, and it will not be an empty and meaningless economic exercise of exchange of time or material for capital.

So, where do I go from here? The answer is that I don't know; the beautiful part is that I am ok with it as I realize I am not meant to know. All I aspire to is to have 100% accord between my three levels of integrity, as previously explained, and enjoy the view from the passenger seat. I no longer have anything to prove; I know I am great at what I do, and frankly, I couldn't care less what society thinks of me at every level. These letters testify to the copious amount of self-development I have endured over decades of trial and error. What you can see from the outside looking in is a fraction of the being inside, not too different from seeing a floating iceberg. I have often experienced real magic, mostly when not looking for it. People, opportunities, and places showed up where there was none. I invite you through this letter to trust that greater forces are dictating the outcome of your life that you or I can understand. I am placing my experiences for all to see an alternate means to the know-how of existence in the magical ride called life.

Transforming into the Void

The Advantages of Shattering Self-Concepts

The power of a blank piece of paper holds the potential to change the world. There is no more potent instrument that humanity has created that encapsulates the essence of the human spirit. The resemblance between the two is genuinely striking. As the paper becomes alive and meaningful through its words and content, it shapes the reader and the world around it with its encapsulated ideas. So does the human spirit as it adorns itself with the identifications of the Ego. Yet, there comes a stage in every Soul's development where the entrapment generated by the identity becomes too small and too narrow, and cracks begin to form as the unfulfilled divine destiny pulls at the very fabric of the essence of the individual. This stage has immense potential, where the self-concept is shattered, and the individual can embark on self-discovery and personal growth. Lessons steer us toward the realization that there must be more to our lives than the simple material aspects, titles, and roles we play with one another.

The beauty is that, unlike paper, which once written upon is hard to erase, the human condition boasts the superpower of the Spiritual Realm as an overlay. This can swiftly create a new being within the self if one steps aside and spawns the conditions to see this metamorphosis through. In a process comparable to a caterpillar becoming a butterfly, the Spirit within the human body can embrace its genuine identity, a blank slate for the Divine to manifest into this world. When we empty ourselves of our personalities, we can tap into the condition called *"flow."* Most of humanity's masterpieces, scientific discoveries, and intellectual realizations have been conceived within this state of conscious awareness. Through emptying ourselves, we finally give way to the creation of our true purpose within our lives. Pursuing simplicity and detachment, we arrive at our true destiny within the totality of a spectrum of possibilities. There is no right or wrong in this masterfully woven tapestry of life. Ultimately, the illusion allows us to experience what we understand as *"free will."* For the vast majority, this mirror through which we exert our egos into the forceful creation of our identities will be the only state of being they know for many lifetimes.

Yet the purpose of this passage is to open the possibility to a completely different means of existence, one in which we learn how to co-create with the Divine within us. In this communion with our Heavenly Father, we mature in our spirituality and realize that there must be a greater purpose for us to walk this earth than simply to play like little children in our small sandboxes. An ordinary life is understandably well-lived, but how many of you reading this have attained everything you once wanted? How many of you have delved deep into the core of your Being and are exceptionally proud of who you have become? I am sure many have had an extraordinary life and achieved remarkable accomplishments. But I am also confident that no human can attain perfection in its entirety unless there is a perfection that is solely attainable by communion with the Spirit and allowing it to reshape us into what our Divine Self was always meant to become in the present lifetime.

We may commence this transformative journey by surrendering our egos, accepting ourselves, and loving our Heavenly Father unconditionally. But one must first clean the house to get to the incomprehensible destiny that awaits. We all carry several skeletons deep inside the closet of our Being. We must stop and take account of the unseen aspects of ourselves that are not in unity with our existence's intended purpose. There is no shortlist for me to pinpoint, as the list is as long and diverse as every human's ability to exert free will. But don't worry; your innate compass deep within you will point the way for you to start shedding the aspects of your identity that no longer serve you. I have undergone several of these mutations over the past few decades ever more rapidly as each growth cycle accelerates, and my Being becomes more congruent with the Divine Blueprint for my Soul and its journey.

Many questions may arise from these points, but the most straightforward answers are always the best. Just let go; you do not need to know all the answers; let life happen for you instead of trying to will it into existence. The beauty of magic is not in understanding how the trick works. The beauty of Divine Manifestation is that there is absolutely nothing impossible for God, and it has been known since the beginning of time what choices are available for us to make and which ones we will eventually choose that will lead us to our destinies. For us, time occurs linearly, but the Ethereal exists inter-dimensionally outside the time-space constraints of our bodies. Although quantum mechanics approaches some aspects of how the observer can alter matter, it doesn't even scratch the surface of what matter is and how consciousness and the Divine can interact with it. But I tell you through my gnostic experiences that the Divine Spark within each one of us contains the totality of the Being within it and that the whole universe bows at its presence once activated.

So, instead of wandering through life, placing deadlines, targets, goals, and achievements, I invite you to explore a paradigm shift. It is one in which you surrender all your doings to become your real Being instead. In this new way, you will engage with the day-to-day affairs of life and work. Still, rather than being solely responsible for the performance, you become the observer who is called to the stage to perform everything as an act of unconditional love from your heart, detaching from the outcome. In this new way of co-creating, you enlist the hidden powers within your Being that take you to a new level of mastery. The result will likely be 100 times better than anything you imagined or prayed for.

In the end, it's time you realize that our Heavenly Father loves us unconditionally, and once we allow Him to take control of our lives, everything improves. Become like a blank piece of paper and let the Holy Spirit be the Sacred Scribe that inscribes your destiny within you - a destiny that your Ego is incapable of even beginning to understand, let alone decipher how to achieve.

What have you been struggling with lately? Release it, let it go. Simply look up to the heavens and say: "*Father, I know I haven't heard from you in a while; sorry for being so tuned into my little sandbox. What would you have me do with this matter? I surrender it to you; please take care of it and guide me to the highest possible outcome for my Being. Thank you.*"